Table of Contents

Acknowledgements

We would like to thank the many people who provided important contributions, support and direct assistance during the production of this book.

Also the many managers with whom we have been in contact throughout the development of this book, their input and insight is greatly appreciated.

In addition we are very grateful to our colleagues in Phoenix Safety for their work and professional contributions during the production of this book.

We would also like to thank those who read the script to ensure accuracy throughout the book's development.

Finally, we would like to thank our editor Frank Scott-Lennon for his unremitting encouragement and patience during the creation of this book.

Adrian Flynn & John Shaw

December 2008

Foreword

Safety Matters! treats all of the elements of current Best Practice in Health & Safety at work.

It is a very welcome addition to our developing series of Human Resource, Organisation Behaviour and General Management Books.

All of the books in the series aim to capture the essentials for busy managers; essential knowledge and skill presented in an *accessible easy-to-read style.*

A list of books already published within the series appears on the inside of the back cover; our website www.ManagementBriefs.com lists forthcoming titles.

You the reader are very important to us and we would welcome any contact from you; it will only improve our products and our connection to our reader population.

Frank Scott-Lennon
Series Editor
frank@ManagementBriefs.com

December 2008

1 Health & Safety Management Systems (SMS)

Chapter outline
Health & Safety Management Systems (SMS)

→ Introduction
→ Policy
→ Organising – the 4 Cs
→ Planning and Implementing
→ Measuring Performance
→ Reviewing Performance and Auditing
→ Summary

Introduction

Most organisations have management systems for one or more aspects of management, for example, Quality Management System ISO IS EN 9001 or Environmental Management System ISO IS EN 14001. A number of Safety Management systems are available, all based on a 'plan, check, act, review' style of management.

In this chapter we will examine a Safety Management System (SMS), and how such a system should be applied within organisations.

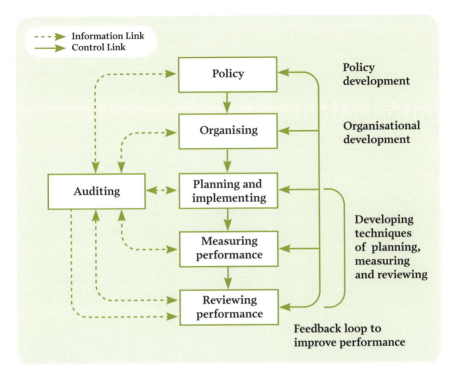

❶ Policy

A well written, current Safety Policy is the foundation of any SMS and unless you know what is in your organisation's safety policy, you will not be in the best position to help in its successful implementation. As a manager, the Safety Policy is your 'bible' for managing safety. It is your role to ensure that the people reporting to you have read and fully understood the policy content.

The Safety Policy must be:

→ Specific to the organisation and the nature of its activities

→ Concise, clearly written, dated and made effective by the signature of the most senior accountable person in the organisation

→ Communicated and readily accessible to all persons at their place of work

→ Reviewed for continuing suitability

→ Made available to relevant external interested parties, when required

The policy should include, as a minimum, the following key principles and objectives to which the organisation is committed:

(i) Protecting the safety and health of all members of the organisation by preventing work-related injuries, ill health, diseases and incidents

(ii) Complying with relevant national laws and regulations, voluntary programs, collective agreements on Health and Safety and other requirements to which the organisation subscribes

(iii) Ensuring that workers and their representatives are consulted and encouraged to participate actively in all elements of the SMS

(iv) Continually improving the performance of the SMS

Ideally, the SMS should be compatible with and integrated into other management systems in the organisation, such as Project Management, Quality Management and Performance Management systems.

2 Organising

The employer should provide leadership for Health & Safety activities in the organisation.

Structures and processes should be established which:

→ Ensure that safety is a line-management responsibility which is known and accepted at all levels

→ Define and communicate to the members of the organisation the responsibility, accountability and authority of persons who identify, evaluate or control safety hazards and risks

→ Provide effective supervision, as necessary, to ensure the protection of workers' safety and health

→ Promote co-operation and communication among members of the organisation, including workers and their representatives, to implement the elements of the SMS

→ Fulfil the principles of SMS contained in relevant national guidelines, tailored guidelines or voluntary programs, as appropriate, to which the organisation subscribes

→ Establish and implement a clear policy and measurable objectives

→ Establish effective arrangements to identify and eliminate or control work-related hazards and risks, and promote health at work

→ Establish prevention and health promotion programs

→ Ensure effective arrangements for the full participation of workers and their representatives in the fulfilment of the policy

→ Provide appropriate resources to ensure that persons responsible for safety, including the safety and health committee, can perform their functions properly

→ Ensure effective arrangements for the full participation of workers and their representatives in safety and health committees, where they exist

We can split 'organising' into what are known as the '4 Cs',

→ Co-operation

→ Communication

→ Control

→ Competence

Co-operation — It has long been recognised that good safety performance depends on everyone co-operating. True co-operation means that you consult your team on the issues that affect their health and safety, such as hazard identification and controls, safe working procedures and the use of Personal Protective Equipment (PPE). As a manager you will have to create the sort of environment in which co-operation is possible. There are 3 important points to assist you in doing this:

ⓘ Consult and agree — when risks are identified, consult with the people exposed to risk and agree on controls which meet everyone's requirements

ⓘⓘ Do what you said you would — not fulfilling your side of an agreement not only has a detrimental effect on the agreement involved but makes it harder to reach agreement in the future.

ⓘⓘⓘ Respond positively — when you are approached on safety matters, respond positively and take action. If you do not, you demonstrate to your team that safety is a low priority for you. Soon people will stop raising safety matters.

Communication — It may seem obvious that there can be no true co-operation without effective communication. In workplaces where true co-operation is in place and working, there will be on-going informal communication on safety matters. However there is also a need for formal communication via Safety Representatives and Safety Committees. Safety Representatives are members of the workforce who voluntarily take on the task of representing the interests of their colleagues on health and safety matters; they are most often chosen by their colleagues. Safety Representatives usually engage in activities such as safety inspections and accident investigations but also play a pivotal role in communication and consultation between management and employees. As a manager you should know who your organisation's Safety Representative is and talk to him or her on a regular basis about safety matters.

Safety Committees are the most formal means of communication on safety matters. The purpose of a safety committee is to

ⓘ Monitor safety performance

ⓘⓘ Suggest remedial actions where necessary

ⓘⓘⓘ Discuss ways of improving the organisation's safety management system.

As a manager it is important that you demonstrate your interest in safety by communicating with the people for whom you are responsible. You can do this by asking questions on safety issues and by passing on information on safety matters, such as recently identified hazards or learning points from accidents in other parts of the organisation. As a manager you must always facilitate the work of Safety Representatives and Safety Committees. You can do this by providing Safety Representatives with time to carry out their duties and by encouraging staff to read committee minutes.

Control – This is an important management issue insofar as, without effective management control, no organisation can continue to effectively operate their SMS. If an employee fails to comply with a safety rule, such as not wearing required safety PPE and you, as a manager, turn a blind eye, then you have failed the SMS. What you must never do as a manager is ignore the safety arrangements as this sends a totally wrong message to the perpetrator and can be very de-motivating for others. Failure to control will also contribute to a weakening of the Safety Culture that one should be trying to cultivate.

Competence – The necessary competence to manage health and safety should be defined by the employer; this to include arrangements being established and maintained to ensure that all persons are competent to carry out the safety and health aspects of their duties and responsibilities.

Managers should have sufficient competence to identify and eliminate or control work-related hazards and risks, and to implement the SMS.

All employees and management must be 'safety competent' so that they can work safely. The main problem with competence is that we do not always realise that we need specialist skills or knowledge. For example, you cannot tell that a chemical is carcinogenic by simply looking at it – you may not even know what carcinogenic means; and even if you do you may not have the knowledge or skills needed to work with it safely. Because of this, organisations should provide employees with information, instruction and training as well as posting relevant safety signage in risk areas.

Panel 1.1

Training programs should:

→ Cover all members of the organisation

→ Be conducted by competent persons

→ Provide effective and timely initial and refresher training at appropriate intervals

→ Include participants' evaluation of their comprehension and retention of the training

→ Be reviewed periodically

→ Be documented, as appropriate and according to the size and nature of activity of the organisation

Training should be provided to all participants at no cost to them and should take place during working hours, if possible.

❸ Planning and implementing

Planning is an important tool in many aspects of management and safety management is no exception. Safety management need not be onerous — but neither should it be seen as something 'additional' to usual management activity. In a well-oiled SMS, most management activity involves risk assessment and active monitoring.

The purpose of planning should be to create an SMS that supports:

i Compliance with national laws and regulations, as the minimum

ii The elements of the SMS

iii Continual improvement in safety performance.

Arrangements should be made for adequate and appropriate planning. These planning arrangements should contribute to the protection of safety and health at work, and should include:

→ A clear definition, priority setting and quantification of the SMS objectives

→ The preparation of a plan for achieving each objective, with defined responsibility and clear performance criteria indicating what is to be done by whom and when

→ The selection of measurement criteria for confirming that the objectives are achieved

→ The provision of adequate resources, including human and financial resources and technical support, as appropriate

❹ Measuring performance

Performance measurement is an essential element of the health and safety management system. The primary purpose is to enable organisations to learn by experience and use these lessons to improve their health and safety management performance.

Procedures to monitor, measure and record safety performance on a regular basis should be developed, established and periodically reviewed. Responsibility, accountability and authority for monitoring at different levels in the management structure should be allocated.

The selection of performance indicators should be according to the size, nature and activity of the organisation and the SMS objectives. Both qualitative and quantitative measures should be considered, even though one has to work harder to devise good qualitative measures. Such measures should:

ⓘ Be based on the organisation's identified hazards and risks, the commitments in the policy and the objectives

ⓘⓘ Support the organisation's evaluation process, including the management review

ⓘⓘⓘ Performance monitoring and measurement should

– Be used as a means of determining the extent to which policy and objectives are being implemented and risks are controlled

– Include both active and reactive monitoring, and not be based only upon work-related injury, ill health, disease and incident statistics

– Be recorded

Monitoring should be a continuous process in good safety management and we will treat the essentials of active and reactive monitoring in chapters 4 & 5.

❺ Reviewing performance and Auditing

As a manager, you should conduct reviews regularly and cover all aspects of health and safety. Your usual employee performance reviews should include health and safety as part of the criteria.

Panel 1.2

Checklist:
Areas for inclusion in Safety Audits

→ Policy

→ Worker participation

→ Responsibility and accountability

→ Competence and training

→ SMS documentation

→ Communication

→ System planning, development and implementation

→ Prevention and control measures

→ Management of change

→ Emergency prevention, preparedness and response

→ Procurement

→ Contracting

→ Performance monitoring and measurement

→ Investigation of work-related injuries, ill health, diseases and incidents, and their impact on safety and health performance

→ Audit procedures

→ Management review

→ Preventive and corrective action

→ Continual improvement

→ Any other audit criteria or elements that may be appropriate.

If you do not conduct general performance reviews then you should arrange for safety reviews to take place on a regular basis with each employee.

Auditing is the process of obtaining a systematic and independent view of the health and safety performance of your organisation. Since auditing must be independent, you cannot audit your own performance in your own area. Often internal audit teams are formed within an organisation; members of these teams audit the safety management of other areas.

The audit conclusions should determine whether the implemented SMS:

1. Is effective in meeting the policy and objectives

2. Is effective in promoting full worker participation

3. Responds to the results of performance evaluation and previous audits

4. Enables the organisation to achieve compliance with relevant national legislation

5. Fulfils the goals of continual improvement and best practice

Summary of Chapter 1

→ A well written Safety Policy is the foundation of any SMS

→ Good safety organisation includes the '4 Cs'

  — Co-operation

  — Communication

  — Control

  — Competence

→ Good planning is an important tool in safety management

→ Systems should be established to ensure that performance measures are in place for safety

→ Safety procedures should be regularly reviewed and audited

Health & Safety
Risk Management

2

Chapter outline
Health & Safety Risk Management

→ Introduction
→ Definitions
→ Basic Risk Management Model
→ What is Risk Assessment?
→ Recording Risk Assessments
→ Management Review of Risk Assessments
→ Summary

Introduction

Effective risk management involves identifying all of the hazards in the workplace, and then carrying out a risk assessment for each hazard, to assess the severity of a risk, before deciding its priority. It will involve achievable steps to protect people from risks that may cause harm or suffering.

Definitions

Risk management incorporates a full range of control measures that may be used to limit, reduce, or eliminate the probability that an undesirable outcome will occur. Risk management also includes control measures that can be used to limit, reduce, or eliminate anticipated hazards, even if the event does not occur. An employer has an obligation to identify and assess foreseeable hazards. If it is not reasonably practicable to eliminate the risk, the employer must take steps to control the risk.

Risk is the combination of the likelihood and the impact of a specified hazardous event.

A risk therefore always has two elements:

→ The likelihood that the hazard will fulfil its potential

→ The impact of the hazardous event

Hazard is anything (situation, source, process or item) that has the potential to kill, or cause injury, ill-health, harm to an individual, damage to property, damage to equipment, damage to the environment or a combination of these.

A **Risk Assessment** is simply a careful examination of what, in your work, could cause harm to people, so that you can weigh up whether you have taken enough precautions or should do more to prevent harm.

Risk Rating: The magnitude of the risk associated with the hazard can be calculated and compared to others, if we allocate numerical scales to the likelihood and impact.

Depending on the methodology adopted, a rating scale is used to identify the high risk activities and therefore corrective action and control measures can be prioritised.

Controlling Risk means that the employer does all that is reasonably practicable to ensure that a hazard will not injure anyone (e.g. by eliminating the hazard, enclosing it in a totally enclosed container, using general or local exhaust ventilation, implementing safe operating procedures, or providing personal protection as a last resort).

The purpose of Risk Management is to: (1) Eliminate Risks, or (2) Reduce them to an 'acceptable' level.

Identification of risk is usually completed using a Risk

Panel 2.1

Risk Management Process

→ **Identifying any foreseeable hazard** – Anything in the workplace that has potential to harm anyone at the workplace, eg moving parts in machinery, toxic chemicals, and manual handling tasks

→ **Assessing the risk from the hazard** – Finding out how significant the risk is e.g. will it cause a serious injury, illness or death and how likely is this to occur?

→ **Eliminating the hazard or if this is not possible, controlling the risk from the hazard** – Implementing strategies to eliminate or control the hazard e.g. design equipment differently, add machine guards, use safer chemicals, providing lifting devices to minimize manual handling or use personal protective equipment

→ **Reviewing risk assessment** – To monitor and improve control measures and find safer ways of doing things

Assessment. An assessment is completed using many different methods designed to quantify the degree of risk created by a machine, situation or activity. This creates a form of prioritisation for action to be taken in relation to those risks.

Basic Risk Management Model

Every organisation is continuously exposed to an endless number of new or changing threats and vulnerabilities that may affect its operation or the fulfillment of its objectives. Identification, analysis and evaluation of these threats and vulnerabilities are the only way to understand and measure the impact of the risk involved and hence to decide on the appropriate measures and controls to manage them.

What is Risk Assessment?

A Risk Assessment is simply a careful examination of what, in your work, could cause harm to people, so that you can weigh up whether you have taken enough precautions or should do more to prevent harm. Workers and others have a right to be protected from harm caused by a failure to take reasonable control measures.

Accidents and ill health can ruin lives and affect your business too if output is lost, machinery is damaged, insurance costs increase or you have to go to court. There is a legal requirement to assess the risks in your workplace so that you put in place a plan to control the risks.

If, as an employer, you have identified a hazard you must assess how dangerous it is. The level of significance of the risk will determine the priority assigned to its elimination or control action taken to eliminate the risk, or, if that is not practicable, control the risk of harm occurring.

An employer must:

→ Evaluate the likelihood of an injury or illness occurring and the likely severity of any injury or illness

→ Review all available health and safety information relevant to the hazard (for example, information from the supplier of plant, material safety data sheets)

→ Identify factors that contribute to the risk (for example, layout and condition of working environment; capability, skill, experience and age of people ordinarily doing the work; systems of work being used and reasonably foreseeable abnormal conditions)

→ Identify actions necessary to eliminate or control the risk

→ Identify any records necessary to be kept to ensure that risks are eliminated or controlled (including how long they should be kept)

Hazard Identification

The starting point in the Risk Assessment Process is to identify the hazards. The hazards may be wide ranging such as building design, access/egress, equipment, clients, contractors, chemicals among others. Hazards can also be categorised into:

◆ **Physical:** Falls, Fire, Electricity, Equipment, Manual Handling

◆ **Chemical:** Glues, solvents, dyes, acids can have short medium or long term effects

◆ **Biological:** Tuberculosis, Hepatitus, Viruses, Legionella

➡️ **Human factor:** Young workers, pregnant employees, people who are physically or mentally challenged

➡️ **Psychosocial:** Stress, bullying, fatigue, shift work, long hours, difficult targets to be met.

Methods for identifying hazards

The first step in control of a hazard is to identify and list them. There are many methods which are useful for identifying hazards, including:

→ Injury and illness records - review employees' data and check the incidence, mechanism and agency of injury, and the cost to the organisation. These statistics can be analysed to alert the organisation to the presence of hazards

→ Staying informed on trends and developments in workplace health and safety, for example via the internet or Health and Safety publications

→ Reviewing the potential impact of new work practices or equipment introduced into the workplace in line with legislative requirements

→ Doing walk-through surveys, inspections or safety audits in the workplace to evaluate the organisation's health and safety system

Panel 2.2

Assess who might be harmed and how

When assessing the risks, it is essential that we look at who might be harmed from the hazards and how this may occur. This will aid in determining the best way to manage the risk.

→ Some workers have particular requirements, for example new and young workers, new or expectant mothers and people with disabilities may be at particular risk. Extra thought will be needed for potential hazards with these categories of people, among others.

→ Cleaners, visitors, contractors, maintenance workers who may not be in the workplace all the time

→ Members of the public, if they could be hurt by activities of your employees

→ If you share your workplace, you will need to think about how your work affects others present, as well as how their work affects your staff — talk to them

→ Considering safety implications when analysing work processes

→ Investigating workplace incidents and `near miss' reports - in some cases there may be more than one hazard contributing to an incident

→ Getting feedback from employees can often provide valuable information about hazards, because they have hands-on experience in their work area

→ Consulting with employees, health and safety representatives and committee members

→ Benchmarking against or liaising with similar workplaces.

Risk Assessment

When you identify a hazard, the next step is to do a Risk Assessment. A Risk Assessment process means you:

→ Gather information about each identified hazard

→ Consider the number of people exposed to each hazard and the duration of the exposure

→ Use the information to assess the likelihood and consequence of each hazard

→ Use a risk assessment table to work out the risk associated with each hazard.

Panel 2.3

Factors for consideration

You should consider the following factors during the risk assessment process:

→ The nature of the hazard posing the risk

→ Combinations of hazards

→ Types of injuries or illnesses foreseeable from exposure

→ The consequences of duration and exposure to the hazard

→ Workplace and workstation layout

→ Working posture and position

→ Work organisation

→ The introduction of new work processes

→ Skill and experience level of employees

→ Personal characteristics of employees exposed to the risk (for example colour blindness or hearing impairment)

→ Existing control measures in place such as the use of clothing and personal protective equipment.

Risk Analysis

One method of assessing risks is to use a risk assessment table. Record the risk rating (Likelihood x Severity) for each hazard you have identified. Below is an example of a risk matrix using a scale of 1-3 for likelihood and severity. Assessments of likelihood and consequence can be translated into levels of risk using a Risk Assessment table. Areas of high risk can be given first priority for elimination or control in the workplace.

Both the likelihood and the severity of a hazard is on a scale of 1 to 3 where one multiplies the figures for both to give a risk rating, which will be between 1 and 9. This will indicate the risk level and timetable required by management to eliminate or reduce the risk level. See table below.

➡ **Trivial Risk:** No further action required

➡ **Tolerable Risk:** No additional risk control/reduction measures required

➡ **Moderate Risk:** Further risk control/reduction measures should be considered and implemented where possible. Hazards graded as Moderate Risk must be closely managed

➡ **Substantial Risk:** Further risk control/reduction measures must be identified. If the risk cannot be reduced further then the hazard must be strictly managed and the frequency and duration of the hazard must be reduced to as low a level as practicable along with the number of persons exposed to the hazard

➡ **Intolerable Risk:** All work involving this hazard is prohibited

Control the Risks

The correct course of action once a hazard is identified is to use control measures. These generally fall into three categories. You can

→ Eliminate the hazard

→ Minimise the risk

	Severity	Slightly Harmful (1)	Harmful (2)	Extremely harmful (3)
	Highly unlikely (1)	Trivial Risk	Tolerable Risk	Moderate Risk
Likelihood	Unlikely (2)	Tolerable Risk	Moderate Risk	Substantial Risk
	Likely (3)	Moderate Risk	Substantial Risk	Intolerable Risk

→ Use controls such as PPE when all other options have been exhausted.

The best way to control a hazard is to eliminate it. The elimination of a hazard is the first choice in a system called the `hierarchy of controls'.

Panel 2.4

Hierarchy of controls

There is an order of priority in hazard control. In relation to specific risks that have been identified and assessed. We should work our way down through the hierarchy below, each stage of which we will treat in turn:

→ Eliminate the hazard

→ Substitute or modify the hazard

→ Isolate the hazard

→ Use engineering methods

→ Use management/ administrative controls

→ Introduce Personal Protective Equipment (PPE)

Elimination

Where no hazard exists, no risk of injury or illness exists. Thus it is always better to go for elimination.

Examples of successful elimination would be:

→ Remove trip hazards in a cluttered corridor

→ Dispose of unwanted chemicals

→ Eliminate hazardous plant or processes

→ Repair damaged equipment promptly

→ Ensure new equipment meets the ergonomic needs of users

Minimising the Risk

Substitution

If it is not possible to eliminate the hazard, substitute it with something - preferably of a lesser risk - which will still perform the same task in a satisfactory manner. For example

→ Substitute a hazardous chemical with a less dangerous one

→ Replace telephone handsets with headsets where there is frequent use of telephone

→ Substitute a less hazardous material to control a vapour hazard

→ Substitute a smaller package or container to reduce the risk of manual handling injuries such as back strain

Modification

Change the plant or system of work to reduce hazards. For example:

→ Re-design plant to reduce noise levels

→ Use a scissors-lift trolley to reducing bending while lifting

→ Install ventilation in chemical storage areas to remove vapours

Management must take responsibility for ensuring that all necessary safety controls are in place.

Isolation

Isolate the problem from staff. This is often done by using separate, purpose-built rooms, barricades or sound barriers. This moves the hazardous process away from the main work area to a site where emissions can be controlled. For example

→ Isolate and store chemicals properly by using a fume cupboard

→ Isolate copying equipment and other machinery in soundproof rooms to reduce exposure to fumes and noise

→ Use security measures to protect staff for example using a swipe card system to limit access to certain hazardous areas.

Panel 2.5

Engineering controls

If you cannot eliminate a hazard or make a substitution to eliminate it, then reduce the chance of hazardous contact. Re-design equipment, work processes or tools to reduce or eliminate the risk. For example

→ Ensure proper machine guarding is in place

→ Use anti-glare screens on computer VDUs

→ Use mechanical aids to minimise manual handling injuries

→ Use ventilation to remove chemical fumes and dusts and/or use wetting down techniques to minimise dust levels

→ Change bench heights to reduce bending

→ Ensure ergonomic factors are taken into account.

Management/Administrative controls

Management must take responsibility for ensuring that all necessary safety controls are in place through: training, job rotation, maintenance of plant and equipment, limitation of exposure time, and the provision of written work procedures. For example

→ Regularly maintain plant and equipment

→ Re-design jobs

→ Use team lifting

→ Limit exposure time to a hazard through staff rotation

→ Train and educate staff to:

  — Identify and assess risks

  — Use methods of control

  — Apply legislative requirements

  — Implement safe manual handling techniques

  — Safely use mechanical aids and equipment

Personal protective equipment

Personal protective equipment (PPE) should only be used as a last resort. PPE is for short term solutions only. PPE protects an employee's body from hazards. PPE must be provided free of charge and maintained by the employer. Employers are also required to ensure that workers are trained in the proper use of PPE.

Employees have a responsibility to use PPE in accordance with their training and safe usage requirements. For example

→ Wear earplugs in noisy areas

→ Wear eye protection when working with hazardous chemicals

→ Wear gloves to protect against infection

Specific controls to reduce risks

Select controls from as high up the hierarchy table as you can. The `elimination' method is the safest solution. In many cases you may need a combination of controls to reduce the level of risk with any one hazard. For example when looking at exposure to hazardous chemicals one could initiate a number of risk reduction strategies from different levels of the hierarchy, such as:

→ Workplace design changes or task modification

→ Substituting an extremely hazardous chemical with a less hazardous one

→ Using a fume cupboard when handling the chemical

→ Ensuring exposure time is limited

→ Providing PPE to employees

Reducing risk to an acceptable minimum will ensure optimum risk reduction for all.

Reducing Risk - ALARP (As Low As Reasonably Practicable)

Ideally we should aim for the total elimination of all risks from the workplace. If this cannot be achieved, then we have to reduce the risk to an acceptable level. To do this we must make a balanced judgement about the risk rating against the time, trouble, resources and cost of the steps needed to remove or reduce it. Remember there is no such thing as total safety. The purpose of risk assessment is to implement control measures to reduce any existing unacceptable risk ratings down to an acceptable or low level. This principle is known as the **ALARP** principle. **As Low As Reasonably Practicable**.

For a risk to be ALARP it must be possible to demonstrate that the cost involved in reducing the risk further would be grossly disproportionate to the benefit gained. The ALARP principle arises from the fact that it may not be possible to spend infinite time, effort and money attempting to reduce a risk to zero. It should not be understood as simply a quantitative measure of benefit against detriment. It is more a best common practice of judgement of the balance of risk and societal benefit.

In essence, making sure a risk has been reduced to a level that is ALARP is about weighing the risk against the sacrifice needed to further reduce it. The decision is weighted in favour of health and safety because the presumption is that the duty-holder should implement the risk reduction measure. To avoid having to make this sacrifice, the duty-holder must be able to show that it would be grossly disproportionate to the benefits of risk reduction that would be achieved. Thus, the process is not one of balancing the costs and benefits of measures but, rather, of adopting measures except where they are ruled out because they involve grossly disproportionate sacrifices.

Extreme examples might be:

→ To spend €2m to prevent 5 staff suffering bruised knees is obviously grossly disproportionate; but

→ To spend €2m to prevent a major chemical explosion capable of killing 150 people is obviously proportionate.

Of course, in reality many decisions about risk and the controls that achieve ALARP are not so obvious. Factors come into play such as on-going costs set against remote chances of one-off events, or daily expense and supervision time required to ensure that, for example, employees wear ear defenders set against a chance of developing hearing loss at some time in the future. It requires judgment. There is no simple formula for computing what is ALARP.

Management Review of Risk Assessments

The workplace is constantly changing. This constant changing

Panel 2.6

Recording Risk Assessments

It is good practice to record the results of risk assessments although detailed records may not be necessary where risks are found to be trivial or when the risk assessment can be repeated easily. It is preferable to use a form for recording risk assessments since this acts as a memory aid for what has to be recorded, in addition to providing a convenient method of structuring the information recorded. There is no definitive structure to recording risk assessments. Generally the assessments are recorded on paper but there are computer programmes available to record and analyse the data collected. The following should be included in any record form:

1. Details of the risk assessors – Name, Job Title

2. Date and time of the assessment

3. Details on what, where, who was assessed (location, equipment etc)

4. Any hazards identified

5. Risk rating for each hazard without risk control in place

6. Risk rating with existing controls in place

7. Further controls that may be required

8. A risk rating where the additional risk controls are to be implemented

9. A review date for the next assessment.

will introduce some new risks and may possibly reduce or remove other existing ones. It makes sense therefore, to review what you are doing on an on-going basis.

It is good practice to review your assessment periodically to be sure that nothing has changed and that your previous risk assessments were complete and accurate, as well as finding out if control methods are effective. Circumstances that may warrant a review can also include:

→ The start of a new project

→ A change in the work process or flow

→ A change or addition to tools, equipment, machinery (including locations or the way they are used)

→ New employees

→ Moving to a new building or work area

→ Introduction of new chemicals or substances

→ When new information becomes available about a current product/task

→ Where an accident/incident has occurred

It may be easy to forget to review risk assessments with all the other aspects of managing a business. It is best practice to set a review date for the risk assessments. This can form part of the risk assessment document and encourage periodic review.

Summary of Chapter 2

→ Risk Management is a tool used by employers to Identify Hazards, Assess the Risks and Implement Review control measures

→ Purpose of risk management is to eliminate risk completely or reduce it to an acceptable level

→ Hazard Identification is the Starting Point of the process — hazards can be categorised into Physical, Chemical, Biological, Human Factor and Psychosocial

→ Once a hazard has been identified, there is a need to assess the risk. It is best to gather as much information as possible on the risk and the people likely to be affected

→ Performing a Risk Analysis will aid in quantifying the risk level. A typical analysis will categorise risk consistent with table on page 21

→ Once risks are quantified — we then must start to generate control measures. The control measures are generally based on a well known Hierarchy of Control — Elimination, Substitution, Isolation, Engineering Control, Management/Administrative Controls and PPE

→ Ideally it would be best to eliminate risks from workplaces, but when not possible the Principle of As Low As Reasonably Practicable (ALARP) should be applied to all risks

→ As the workplace is constantly changing, we must be alert to new risks that may be introduced

Leadership and Organisational Safety Culture

3

Chapter outline
Leadership and Organisational Safety Culture

→ Introduction
→ Definition of Leadership in terms of health and safety
→ 10 Principles of Safety Leadership Behaviour
→ Safety Culture within an organisation
→ Safety Culture and Adverse Events
→ Barriers
→ Assessing Safety Culture
→ Improving Safety Culture
→ Summary

Introduction

It is recognised that leadership is important in the creation of a culture that supports and promotes a strong health and safety performance of an organisation. The Manager and /or the team leader are vital in inspiring employees to a higher level of safety and productivity, which means that they must apply good leadership attributes on a daily basis.

Leadership in terms of health and safety

Ask yourself, do my managers/ team leaders:

→ Communicate safety standards to their teams?

→ Involve them in hazard spotting in the workplace?

→ Prevent unsafe acts?

→ Motivate staff to be safer?

→ Monitor safety standards on a daily basis?

It is important that managers/ team leaders are trained in their key role as safety leaders and that they are free to implement these skills at every level. It is also critical that the application of these safety leadership skills is monitored.

Training managers/team leaders in safety leadership skills and ensuring that they apply them on the job has been proven to greatly aid injury prevention, and can also contribute to quality and productivity improvements.

Creating a good Safety Culture requires a common vision and effort from everyone in an organisation. Research into the subject has demonstrated that the management philosophy of an organisation is the most important factor determining its safety performance; for example organisations with the lowest lost-time injury rates have the highest level of management commitment and employee involvement.

10 Principles of Safety Leadership Behaviour

Clear leadership is one of the top priorities for the establishment of a positive Safety Culture. Here are ten safety leadership principles that a leader should not ignore, and which are likely to promote a positive Safety Culture:

❶ Safety as a Top Priority

In making every business decision there are a number of competing priorities e.g. cost, quality and yield. It is imperative that senior management should give safety a high status in the business objectives, and safety should be prioritised in all situations.

❷ Visible Management Commitment to Safety

This is leading by example. It is important that senior management demonstrate visibility and repeat their commitment to safety throughout all areas of the organisation. For example, if senior management fail to challenge unsafe behaviours they unwittingly reinforce the notion that this behaviour is acceptable to the organisation. Senior management decisions and actions must match their words – this creates a shared vision of the importance of safety to the organisation.

❸ Increasing Visibility around Safety

It is good to develop a habit of personally conducting safety walkabouts. This demonstrates commitment and managers will become personally aware of the real safety conditions in their area. These walkabouts will also provide an opportunity for managers to meet their teams in their work areas and to have proactive discussions regarding safety.

❹ Safety Reporting

A positive Safety Culture requires effective reporting from staff of frontline safety issues and problems e.g. accidents, near misses and safety concerns. Communicating a problem or concern is only one step on the route towards a good Safety Culture. It is important that feedback mechanisms should be in place to respond to the reporter (if required) regarding any actions taken.

Effective safety leaders should respond to all incidents in a positive, learning way. They will lead teams to prompt and thorough investigation of all reports (accidents/incidents/near misses), identifying root causes and implementing corrective actions.

This sends a strong message that knowing about anything that goes wrong is vital to creating the conditions necessary to eliminating the next injury. It also sends a clear message that management view safety performance as important as other business objectives.

❺ Staff Involvement

Active employee participation is a positive step towards preventing and controlling hazards. Ownership for safety can be improved by providing effective training and providing forums for employees which assist in getting them to be personally responsible for areas of safety.

It should be made easy for staff to report concerns about decisions that are likely to affect them and feedback mechanisms should be established.

❻ Create a Learning Culture

All employees should be involved in learning by contributing ideas for improvement, and should be encouraged to become aware of what a good safety performance actually means in terms of their own jobs.

The existence of a learning culture enables the organisation to identify, learn and change unsafe conditions and behaviours.

❼ Provide Recognition

A safety leader will give recognition to the delivery of good safety performance e.g. recognise the achievements of employees who improve safety in the organisation, including those who voluntarily contribute to safety.

❽ An Open Culture

Employees should feel that they are able to report issues or concerns without fear that they will be personally blamed or disciplined as a result. Leaders should demonstrate care and concern towards employees and should have an open door policy in place to demonstrate this.

❾ Effective Communication

Effective communication from management to staff is vital for the success of safety leadership. This can be achieved by:

→ A visible safety policy

→ Emphasis on safety related issues and policies via staff communication systems e.g. memos, newsletters, messages from top management, quarterly reports, annual reports, safety sheets

→ The communication of major accidents

Communication systems should be in place within the organisation for the effective transfer of safety and health information between individuals, departments, work groups and teams.

❿ Safety Management System

Organisations should have effective systems in place for the management and co-ordination of safety. This should be led by the most senior person in the organisation, with the support of the senior management team and safety professionals (if required). Objectives should be set to monitor the performance of the system. Outcomes should be communicated to all staff within the organisation at regular intervals.

Safety Culture within an organisation

The term Safety Culture was introduced by the International Atomic Energy Agency (IAEA) as a result of their first analysis into the nuclear reactor accident at Chernobyl:

The Safety Culture of an organisation is the product of the individual and group values, attitudes, perceptions, competencies and patterns of behaviour that determine the

Safety Culture

"The product of individual and group values, attitudes, perceptions, competencies and patterns of behaviour that can determine the commitment to, and the style and proficiency of an organisation's health and safety management system"

ACSNI Human Factors Study Group, HSC (1993)

Psychological Aspects

'How people feel'

Can be described as the **'Safety Climate'** of the organisation, which is concerned with individual and group values, attitudes and perceptions

Behavioural Aspects

'What people do'

Safety-related actions and behaviours

Situational Aspects

'What the organisation has'

Policies, procedures, regulation, organisational structures, and the management systems

commitment to, and the style and proficiency of, an organisation's health and safety management.

Put simply: The way we do things around here on safety! You can judge whether a company has a good Safety Culture from what its employees actually ***do*** rather than what they ***say.***

A large number of factors contribute to whether you have a good or a bad Safety Culture. The list below covers the main factors to indicate whether you have a good Safety Culture:

→ Visible Management commitment

→ Good Safety Communication

→ Safety over Productivity/Profit

→ Learning Organisation

→ High Participation in Safety

→ Sufficient Health and Safety Resources

→ Low Level of Risk-Taking Behaviours

→ Trust between management and frontline staff

→ Good Contractor Management

→ High Levels of Competency

A Safety Culture consists of shared beliefs, practices, and attitudes that exist in an organisation. The culture is the atmosphere created by those beliefs, attitudes etc., which shape our behaviour. Managers/team leaders have a key role to play in developing such a Safety Culture.

Safety Culture and Adverse Events

Well publicised major accidents such as Piper Alpha, Herald of Free Enterprise and Kings Cross Station have highlighted the effect of organisational, managerial and human factors on safety outcomes. Numerous reports of major disasters have identified Safety Culture as a factor that definitely influenced the outcome.

Within the reports of inquiries into such major disasters as the ones mentioned, observations have been made that accidents are not only as a result of human error, environmental conditions or technical failures alone, but also they are as a result of a break down in policies and procedures that were established to manage safety.

Where incidents occur it is important to identify what factors may have contributed to the outcome in order to avoid similar incidents in the future. Common symptoms of poor cultural factors can include:

→ Widespread routine breaking of safety rules

→ Failure to comply with the organisation's own policies

→ Management decisions that appear consistently to put production or cost before safety

→ Managers/Team Leaders not engaging in proactive safety behaviours

In relation to major disasters it is only the final outcomes that are rare and the specific conditions which produced this final outcome. The individual casual factors are usually present in the system all of the time. Removing a single causal factor from a system (e.g. poor Safety Culture), or reducing its frequency, will reduce the likelihood of a disaster occurring.

Sub-cultures

Cultures are not necessarily good or bad, but they are good or bad at achieving certain outcomes. Cultures are learned by their members, so changing the culture requires a lot of discussion, communication and learning.

Changing behaviours is difficult because people have very strong 'patterns' that they follow from habit, and are generally unconscious of their own assumptions. Leaders change culture by holding different assumptions and by making them visible through words and actions.

Sub-cultures are present in every organisation, large and small. In order to change these sub-cultures, there needs to be an understanding of those sub-cultures that may exist. The list below are categorisations of the most common sub-cultures that may exist in an organisation; typically these may exist and differ from department to department or from working group to working group:

1 The Executive Culture

→ Focuses on money, performance, measurement, production, processes, information and abstractions. This is a directing and controlling culture.

2 The Technology Culture

→ Focuses on science, equipment, automation, information technology etc. This culture type tends to want to eliminate the human being as an uncontrolled variable. This type of culture is rational, logical and resists the building of a real 'culture'.

3 The Operating Culture

→ Focuses on making things work, accepting the frustrations of 'the way things are' and can sometimes be seen as a group of people who 'live in the real world'.

4 The Regulatory Culture

→ Focuses on the role of authorities, the role of experts and the role of the public. Other work organisation cultures are influenced by a regulatory culture.

It is important to try to understand the various sub-cultures in one's own organisation, particularly if evaluating a culture change programme.

Barriers

There are a wide range of reasons why some organisations may be reluctant to assess their own level of safety maturity, such as:

→ Not perceiving there to be a need

→ Worries about what might be discovered

→ Resource issues

→ Difficulties associated with signing up to long-term commitments

→ Belief that there is nothing (positive) to achieve

→ Concern that the results of assessments may be markedly worse than those of other groups, sites or competitors

Management/Team Leaders need to overcome the above possible reasons for non-engagement or else it will be impossible to make significant progress.

If the senior management of the organisation are serious about culture change they must work hard to overcome the above barriers.

Panel 3.1

Barriers to Cultural Change

It is important to also recognise that barriers exist to achieving long term cultural change. Here are some examples to the barriers to effective change:

→ Management styles may be different between departments. This may create inconsistencies in the right message been sent

→ There may be weaknesses in the communication interface. Unclear lines of communication may cause confusion and a lack of involvement in the process

→ Management's role in balancing the principles, policies, objectives, and Safety Culture among the functional areas is often constrained by an inability to communicate between the top and bottom of the organisation. The goal should be to make safety a value, not just a priority

→ Organisational bureaucracy may often work against the Safety Culture. Oftentimes routine tasks become the causal factor of human performance errors because they are so routine that employees find ways to cut steps out of the process

→ The formality of procedures and the clear lines of authority also constrain the competitive nature of empowering employees

→ Risk of recruiting people who may not buy in to the organisation's Safety Culture. It is important that all new employees (at every level of the organisation) are trained in a timely manner and gain operating experience to match current employees, thus having negative effects on the Safety Culture

Panel 3.2

Measurable Features of Safety Culture

The following are a list of Safety Culture features that may be measured:

→ Individual values, perceptions, attitudes and behaviours with respect to safety

→ Group values, perceptions, attitudes and behaviours with respect to safety

→ Commitment of management to having safety as a core value, providing resources and visible support to safety programmes

→ Clear mission statement with commonly understood and agreed goals

→ The current safety management system

→ Quality of data from reporting systems

→ The use of reporting systems

→ Quality of training programmes

→ Employee involvement

→ New idea encouragement and capture

→ Accountability of individuals and teams

Assessing Safety Culture

The Safety Culture of an organisation is an important factor in ensuring the effectiveness of risk management. The health and safety related behaviour of individuals in an organisation is influenced by the Safety Culture, and the behaviours in turn determine the culture. Therefore, measuring the Safety Culture should form part of the overall process of measuring the health and safety performance of the organisation.

Because of its indefinable nature, Safety Culture is difficult to observe or measure. In attempting to measure or assess the Safety Culture of an organisation it is necessary to identify what actually constitutes Safety Culture.

Safety Culture assessments should concentrate on the people side of safety, that is measuring the cultural processes that enable the health and safety management system to work — safety behaviours, communication, trust, leadership, commitment, group norms and organisational influences.

In assessing the Safety Culture of the organisation, you can establish where it currently stands and where the culture can be improved and strengthened. Surveys and questionnaires have been commonly used to assess Safety Culture within organisations. Qualitative analysis can also be used, such as group discussions and case studies.

It is important that survey questionnaires are designed to reduce the possibility of bias. When conducting surveys ensure that a representative sample of respondents is achieved and that respondents are allowed to give open and honest responses. Do not repeat a Safety Culture survey unless actions have been achieved from the previous survey.

In conclusion, a Safety Culture assessment can be used as a starting point for change. It will provide the leaders of the organisation a realistic view of the organisation's strengths and weaknesses and this can often trigger real change.

Improving Safety Culture

The following outlines the steps that can be taken to improve the Safety Culture in your organisation:

1 Obtain Top Management Commitment

→ This is vital, and it is very important that it is achieved. If top management in an organisation does not buy into the development of a good Safety Culture, safety will compete against other business elements such as production and costing – this battle will not be won. Top management need to understand the requirement for change and be willing to support it. Being able to show the direct and indirect costs of accidents/incidents can be a compelling argument for change in an organisation.

2 Describe the desired culture in a structured framework

→ Policies, goals and operational plans must be defined. These will guide individuals during the cycle of change, and allow the organisation to remain focused on the improvement process.

3 Build a common understanding of culture

→ It is important that a shared vision for improving safety be established. Top and middle management need to set the example and drive the change process forward demonstrating this shared vision where possible.

4 Assess the existing culture

→ To get where you want to go, you must know where you are starting from. (See our earlier section 'Assessing Safety Culture').

5 Communicate the assessment results

→ Communicating results is an important method of maintaining the effort required for change to happen, and for keeping everyone motivated. Everyone needs to be updated throughout the process. Keep your communication process simple and ensure that everyone involved in the system has a voice, otherwise there will be a reluctance to buy into the process.

6 Identify gaps, root causes and key initiatives to improve

→ Develop an on-going measurement and feedback system. Drive the system with measures that encourage positive change e.g. numbers of hazards reported; numbers of inspections/audits; number of equipment checks; number of safety suggestions reported.

7 Communicate the direction and engage Team leaders and staff

→ The change process will not work if only management know about it. The entire organisation needs to know and be involved in some form or another. All those involved must understand why they are being asked to change what they normally do and what it will look like if they are successful.

→ Awareness training sessions should be held to inform all staff of the new direction the organisation is taking for improving safety standards. Additionally specific Team Leader training courses could be held to ensure that Team Leaders are aware of the practical requirements needed to drive and achieve real change.

8 Implement change

→ This will be achieved via involvement of all interested parties e.g. management, unions (if present), contractors, and employees. The continuous improvement process will include:

i Planning –
The act of identifying opportunities for improvement and identifying ways of achieving these improvements;

ii Doing –
The actual implementation of the actions needed to effect the change;

ⅲ Checking -
The act of verifying whether the implemented changes resulted in the desired improvements; and

ⅳ Action -
What one does in response to the effects observed.

Summary of Chapter 3

→ Strong clear leadership from Management and Team Leaders is essential in creating a Safety Culture within the organisation

→ The Safety Culture describes the management of safety in the workplace, and often reflects the attitudes, beliefs, perceptions and values that employees share in relation to safety

→ Management Commitment, Communication and Competency are examples of a positive Safety Culture

→ Widespread failure to comply with company safety policies and rules creates a Poor Safety Culture

→ Studies have shown that a poor Safety Culture contributes to major accidents

→ Management/Team Leaders need to identify, examine and overcome the barriers to achieving an improved cultural change

→ Improving the Safety Culture will take time and resources. Commitment from Top Management, Communication, Assessing/Improving the existing culture are essential in this process

Proactive Monitoring

4

Chapter outline
Proactive Monitoring

→ Introduction
→ Proactive Monitoring
  – Safety Inspections
  – Safety Inspection Checklist
  – Safety Audits
→ How often?
→ Trend Analysis
→ Summary

Introduction

Monitoring health and safety in the workplace should not be an annual review, it needs to be on-going to ascertain any issues or identify areas that need attention or improvement.

Implementing a Health and Safety Management System in the working environment is the initial step that is taken in the process. Health and safety management requirements change continually and there is a need to be proactive in monitoring the effectiveness of the policy/ system. In real terms, this means being able to identify potential problems and to take action to prevent them becoming reality. There is also a need to be reactive to any breaches or near-breaches of health and safety, by investigating why an incident has occurred, for example.

Panel 4.1

Proactive Monitoring – before accidents happen

Proactive monitoring involves regular inspection and checking to ensure that plans, procedures and controls are being implemented. It is the responsibility of Management and Team Leaders to monitor the effectiveness of the health and safety management functions undertaken by their staff.

Proactive (sometimes termed Active) monitoring provides feedback on safety performance within an organisation before an accident, case of ill-health or an incident. It involves measuring compliance with the performance standards that have been set and achievement against the specific objectives laid down. The primary purpose of proactive monitoring is to measure success and to re-inforce positive achievements in order to nurture a positive Safety Culture. It is not intended as a means of identifying and punishing failure.

Proactive Monitoring can take two forms:

→ Regular **safety inspections** to check that your standards are being implemented and that management controls are working

→ More detailed **safety audits**

This is usually carried out by a manager/team leader and/ or an employee, all of whom would have had some training in identifying hazards and assessing risks. In some cases the Safety Officer or an employee appointed safety representative may also carry out a safety inspection.

Safety Inspections

Inspections are an important element of safety management and are carried out by organisations as a means of assisting in the improvement of their safety performance.

This is a proactive process involving the examination of the workplace, work activities or documentation and comparing it with agreed standards. Inspection can take different forms:

→ Safety tours or ad hoc visits to selected parts or the entire department and are especially effective if carried out by senior departmental managers as this demonstrates their commitment to safety

→ Checklists can be used to examine a specific work area or activity and can be used to identify items for action under specific headings

→ Examining documentation, for example risk assessments or codes of practice, and comparing the standards set with observed practices

→ Risk surveys involve examining the overall management of risk associated with a specific hazard, for example liquid nitrogen, display screen equipment or lasers. The remedial action needed and the person responsible for implementing it should be documented. The results of inspections should be reported to appropriate levels of management who can determine if a review of departmental arrangements is necessary

Inspection reports are a record of how well the department is controlling its risks and where it needs to improve. The results of these reports should be communicated to staff and departmental safety groups or representatives. A written report should be compiled after the inspection. This, together with any supporting information, may need to be referred to those people in your management structure who have the authority to sanction the appropriate remedial action to be taken – particularly where it entails a high level of expenditure or organisational policy changes. In smaller organisations the approach to these inspections can be flexible and need only be as sophisticated as the complexity of your work and the nature of the hazards demand.

Safety Inspection Checklist

It is good practice to use a standard report form for safety inspections.

The form should include:

→ A checklist of the processes, activities and parts of your premises that are to be inspected

→ A section for identifying hazards and potential risks

→ Apace for comments on any remedial action that is recommended or has already been decided upon

→ An agreed timetable for completing the remedial action.

The items in the checklist will depend on your business type. Typical examples would include fire safety, housekeeping, chemical safety and slip, trip and fall hazards.

Safety Inspection Results

The results should be properly recorded and evaluated so that you can assess:

→ Whether the health and safety standards in the organisation remain acceptable

→ The extent to which your company complies with the relevant health and safety legislation — which is often a direct indication of how effectively hazards have been identified, controlled or eliminated

→ Whether standards have improved or deteriorated since the last inspection. This type of monitoring involves a systematic collection of information about the nature and scale of the hazards and it is an important aspect of health and safety performance measurement.

→ Where the risks are greatest so that priority can be given to these areas. Look closely at those with the potential for serious injury or damage — bearing in mind what both the immediate and underlying causes of a possible accident could be.

It is also an opportunity for a critical appraisal of all the elements of your health, safety and welfare arrangements.

Safety Audit

A **safety audit** is a detailed and analytical review of the management of health and safety across all the areas of the organisation. It requires extensive pre-planning, and takes much longer to complete than a safety inspection.

A health and safety professional or a body specialising in safety auditing normally carries out the audit, although a trained internal auditor may also complete audits. The aim is to produce a root-and-branch report assessing:

→ Your company's health and safety policy and rules

→ Whether your company complies with health and safety legislation.

Audit protocols and terms of reference must be agreed in advance of the audit.

The key areas of an audit are typically:

→ Any examples of non-conformance with the company's health and safety policy

→ Any instances of non-compliance with the relevant legislation

→ An action plan to correct the deficiencies.

Issues should be graded according to the degree of severity and, where legislation is not complied with, the degree to which your business is left exposed to the legal process.

How often?

Measuring health and safety performance is an on-going activity, so in one sense the measurement process is continuous. But like any other activity measurement should be both efficient and effective, so the frequency with which it takes place needs to be planned appropriately. You should consider the following factors:

◉ Suitable intervals to ensure that specific planned objectives are achieved

◉ The potential for change from one state to another over time

◉ The relative importance of the activity or particular precaution relative to the overall control of risk

◉ Where intervals for monitoring are prescribed by legislation

◉ Where there is evidence that there is non-compliance

◉ Where there is evidence of compliance

◉ The relative frequency and time at which a particular activity takes place

Trend Analysis

By identifying trends, your organisation can be assured that there is a focus on loss prevention and gain a better understanding of why workplace accidents have occurred.

Analysing trends will help you:

→ Review statistical data to reveal trends, both favourable and unfavourable

→ Identify specific areas on which to concentrate accident prevention efforts

Data to Analyse

It will be useful to focus analyses on the following data:

→ Recordable Injury Records/Logs

→ First Aid Register

→ Safety Inspections

→ Accident/Incident Investigation Reports

→ Employee Hazard Reports

Process of Data Analysis

The process below should be useful for data analysis:

→ Select Data to be analysed

→ Determine a time period to be looked at

→ Identify similarities in the data

→ Develop corrective measures to stop unfavourable trends

→ Continue with effective interventions

Identifying Patterns

Patterns may typically emerge on some of the bases listed below:

→ Same Job Location

→ Same Type of Equipment

→ Time of Day

→ Day of Week

Summary of Chapter 4

→ Proactive Monitoring of the Workplace will monitor the effectiveness of the Company Safety policy and procedures

→ Proactive monitoring should take place on a regular basis and will measure compliance/success and will also help re-inforce a positive Safety Culture

→ Examples of Proactive Monitoring include – Regular Safety Inspections, Detailed Safety Audits, Safety Surveys, Examining Records and Safety Documentation

→ Identifying trends or data such as injury/illness, risk assessments and First Aid treatment administered can assist management to focus on loss prevention and why accidents are occurring

→ Proactive Monitoring must be an on-going process. Management should ensure that it is well planned and takes place regularly

Reactive Monitoring

5

Chapter outline
Reactive Monitoring

Introduction

Reactive monitoring is a response to an accident or incident. Reactive monitoring involves investigating an accident/incident, determining the root cause and facilitating the implementation of the appropriate corrective measures.

Reactive Monitoring

Reactive monitoring measures accidents, cases of ill-health and incidents. The idea being to identify the causes of these failures and to take remedial action which will prevent them occurring again. Whereas information is easier to obtain from serious accidents, it is less easy to obtain from incidents (near misses which could have led to an accident but, fortunately, did not).

Accident Triangle

In 1931, H.W. Heinrich reported on a study of accidents that he classified according to severity. Heinrich's report showed that for each serious-injury incident, we could expect about 29 minor injuries and 300 near-miss or property-damage incidents. His conclusions are often depicted with a pyramid or triangle indicating a single serious incident at the peak and a broad base of non-injury incidents.

These relationships may be accurate for large populations and are often used to stress the importance of paying attention to detail. The concept is that if the small incidents (near misses and property damage incidents) continue to occur unabated, that eventually, an incident resulting in a serious injury will occur. To a certain degree the assumption may be accurate. Oftentimes the

only difference between a near miss and a serious injury is timing — a matter of seconds or inches.

It is therefore essential that every time a near-miss occurs, a thorough investigation is carried out to ascertain the root cause of the incident. Once the cause has been identified, corrective action can be taken, thus reducing the likelihood that a given near-miss will occur again.

By examining the causes of all such outcomes, and by putting in place corrective measures, valuable lessons can be learned from the 'near-misses'. These lessons will help to reduce the possibility that a serious injury may occur.

Incident Reporting and Recording

Incidents can yield positive results if we learn from what went wrong and prevent a re-occurrence. To achieve this we need to investigate the circumstances that led to the incident and report, record, analyse and correct its effects. This requires personnel trained in accident reporting and investigation techniques, which are essential elements of any effective safety management system.

Improving Incident Reporting Process

In general the less serious an incident is, the less likely to be reported. It is essential that an accurate account of what is really happening in the organisation is reported.

In order to improve the reporting of incidents we can:

→ Provide an easy-to-use reporting system

→ Reporting should be encouraged as 'continuous improvement' and 'prevention of re-occurrence'

→ Reporting should not be seen as a 'finger pointing' or 'blame exercise'

→ Show that you are using the data collected

→ Give feedback on the data collected

Accident/incident investigation

An accident/incident for Health and Safety purposes is any unplanned event where:

1. Someone suffers an injury or ill health;

2. Someone could have suffered an injury or ill health or there could have been damage or loss to property if the circumstances had been slightly different (often called a 'near miss' or 'near hit' or dangerous occurrence).

The primary aim of an investigation is to establish the cause of the accident/incident. Knowing the cause of an accident/incident will identify the appropriate action to prevent a recurrence. An investigation is not undertaken to apportion blame for the accident/incident. Such an approach would be unlikely to succeed in determining the cause of the accident/incident since vital information may not be forthcoming.

As much information as possible into the cause of the accident/incident should be gathered so as to:

→ Prevent a similar accident happening

→ Report to the relevant national Enforcing Authority

→ Comply with legal requirement

→ Gather information required to initiate, or defend, an insurance claim.

Immediate action may be required to prevent further accidents before starting the investigation, for example stop an activity or withdraw equipment. Following a serious accident/incident the area where the event occurred should be secured and no one allowed to enter or interfere with it. The Police, relevant Enforcing Authority and other staff may have to examine the area.

55

Panel 5.1

Checklist to Guide the Structure of Investigation & Reports

❶ Obtain basic facts

→ Has anything been damaged since the accident/incident?

→ Names of injured/ill employees/witnesses/people first on the scene

→ Extent of injury/ill health/ damage/disruption

→ The task that was being undertaken at the time of the accident/incident

→ The time, place and layout of area (building, room)

→ The environmental conditions (lighting, ventilation, floor conditions, obstructions and weather conditions, if outside)

→ Record conditions e.g. take photographs or make sketches

❷ Obtain witness statements

→ Name, contact details and occupation of witness

→ What did they observe and how did they react?

❸ Establish circumstances

→ What was being done at the time and what happened?

→ What was the accepted method for carrying out the task? Was that method being followed? Was it adequate?

→ Was the individual competent to carry out the task (qualifications, experience)?

→ What instruction and training was given (records available)?

→ Were they aware of risk assessment for the task (how they could be harmed and the measures they should take to prevent harm)?

→ Had the individuals been told to carry out the task, or were they acting on their own initiative?

→ Has something similar happened previously?

4 Immediate response to accident/incident

→ Was prompt and appropriate action taken (e.g. fire fighting, first aid, spillage procedure, make area safe, restrict access, isolate electricity, warning notices, referral to Occupational Health)?

5 Identify preventative measures

→ Review the risk assessment for the task (copy available)

→ What safety precautions were in place and what safety precautions should have been in place?

→ What instruction and training was given and what instruction and training should have been given?

6 Identify underlying causes

→ Was supervision and training adequate?

→ Was equipment suitable for task?

→ Was equipment maintained and tested adequately?

→ What pressures/constraints, if any, were being applied?

→ Was communication adequate between relevant parties?

7 Actions to prevent a recurrence

→ Could the outcome have been more serious?
→ What needs to be done to prevent similar accident/ incident?

→ Were the safety precautions adequate but not implemented? Why not?

8 Actions to prevent recurrence include:

→ Better guarding or barriers

→ Better test and maintenance schedules

→ Revised work method/Risk Assessment

→ Provision and use of personal protective equipment

→ Improved supervision, training, inspection, instruction and information

→ Better communication

→ Review similar activities elsewhere

One should consider the severity or potential severity of the accident/incident when deciding upon the depth of the investigation. A full and detailed investigation is required for serious accidents: a less detailed one for minor accidents.

What Is The Domino Theory?

Heinrich's Domino Theory states that accidents result from a chain of sequential events, metaphorically like a line of dominoes falling over. When one of the dominoes falls, it triggers the next one, and the next... but removing a key factor (such as an **unsafe condition** or an **unsafe act**) can prevent the start of the chain reaction.

The Domino Theory suggests that if one of the dominoes (representing an element of an accident) falls, this will have a knock on approach on other elements and the end results of all these factors is loss or an accident. For example if a person slipped and fell on wet floor breaking their arm, the sequence of events would be the following:

→ Lack of Supervision (management control) results in a situation where liquid can be spilt and not cleared up

→ An Unsafe Act Occurs — spilling liquid and not cleaning it up

→ Unsafe Conditions Results — pool of oil on the floor

→ Loss/Injury Results — when a person slips in the liquid, falls and breaks an arm.

The most important domino **(The Lack of Management Control)** is the domino that is at the beginning of the whole process and effective action at this stage can provide the opportunity to cut out the probability of a later accident.

Conducting Investigation Interviews

In the majority of investigations, the main source of information will be the people involved. Those people who will be interviewed include:

→ Injured Parties

→ Those who caused injury to property such as equipment/machinery

→ Witnesses to the accident/incident

→ Team Leaders or colleagues of those involved

→ Others who may have contributed to the causes of the accident

Conducting Investigation interviews on site has the major

advantage that interviewees can point to locations, machines etc and not have to describe them. Some verbal descriptions can be difficult to generate and susceptible to misinterpretation. Ideally interviews would be conducted on site but this is not always possible due to the nature of the investigation and site facilities.

Certain problems/issues may arise from the interview process, such as:

➡ **Difficulties in language –** Interviewee's first language may not be English or the first language of the interviewer. This may lead to inaccurate or confusing information being passed from both sides. Translation services should be requested, as needed.

➡ **Poor Communication –** This may occur in persons suffering from shock after the events; in this event the interview should be delayed. In the case where the interviewee has poor communication, the description of the accident may be difficult. The interviewer will have to adapt their technique in order to obtain the necessary information.

➡ **Unwilling to provide information –** Interviewer needs to identify if the interviewee is unwilling or

unable to provide information. The interviewer needs to be able to differentiate between unwillingness and genuine amnesia. If the person is unwilling, we need to differentiate between the underlying causes of this. It may be the fear of disciplinary action, loss of compensation. The interviewer will have to adjust their own individual technique to solve these issues.

➡ **Not providing the accurate information –** The interviewer needs to identify that:

1 Someone is telling untruths, and;

2 Why they are doing this.

There is a need at this point to establish the facts of what happened rather than what the person believed to have happened. If a group of people witness an accident, more than likely they will all provide different descriptions of what happened. They have all given their version of the 'truth' and it certainly cannot be assumed that either of the two individuals are lying just on the basis that they have a different recollection.

Summary of Chapter 5

→ Reactive Monitoring is a management response (after the event) to an accident or incident

→ Reactive Monitoring involves investigating an accident, finding the causes and implementing preventative actions

→ Management must ensure that accident/incident reporting is accurate and timely

→ The purpose of the accident/incident investigation is to identify what occurred, what contributed to it and how can it be prevented from occurring in the future

→ Blaming someone for an accident will not aid the process and vital information may be withheld

→ An accident investigation involves – physically examining the scene, interviewing witnesses and examining all of the facts

→ It is essential to identify the root causes of the accident, but also any underlying contributing environmental/cultural factors

→ When the accident investigation is complete, management must put in place a plan of action to prevent its recurrence and review the actions on a regular basis

→ The Domino Theory Model has been developed as a tool for showing how accidents can occur in organisations

Prevention of Slips, Trips and Falls

6

Chapter outline
Prevention of Slips, Trips and Falls

→ Introduction
→ Movement of People at Work
→ Falls on a level
→ Housekeeping
→ Falls from Height
→ Slips/Trips/Falls Risk Assessment
→ Controls for Slips, Trips and Falls
→ Housekeeping Inspections
→ Summary

Introduction

The movement of people, goods and equipment around any building or site can create hazards which are best addressed by designing suitable traffic routes and installing where necessary signs, guides, barriers and similar devices to reduce the risk of collisions, falls and injuries.

Movement of People at Work

Operations such as moving premises, internal movement of equipment and people can bring additional hazards to traffic routes. If routes are blocked or crowded, they can lead to two main types of accidents:

→ Slips, trips and falls — these are very regular occurrences in workplaces

→ Delay in Emergency Evacuations

Falls on a level

The terms slips, trips and falls are commonly used but not analysed as to where the accidents may occur. Statistics show that a majority of falls occur on the same level.

In general, slips, trips and falls occur due to loss of traction between the shoe and the walking surface or an inadvertent contact with a fixed or moveable object.

Housekeeping

Good housekeeping is very important in relation to preventing slip, trips and falls. If good housekeeping practices are not enforced, other control measures will never be fully effective.

If an organisation's housekeeping habits are poor, the result may

Panel 6.1

Conditions and situations that increase the risk of slips and falls:

→ Poor housekeeping

→ Wet or slippery surfaces

→ Obstacles in walkways

→ Poor lighting

→ Inadequate footwear

→ Individual behaviour

well be employee injuries, ever increasing insurance costs and legal issues. If an organisation's facilities are noticeably clean and well organised, it is a good indication that its overall safety program is effective. In addition to safety, disorderly work environments can negatively impact the morale of employees who must function in a job site that is dirty, hazardous and poorly managed.

According to statistics, workers are injured from slips, trips and falls more than any other occupational hazard. These can often be avoided if proper housekeeping procedures are used.

Panel 6.2

A Housekeeping Safety Checklist/ Programme will examine some of the areas below:

→ Dust and Dirt Removal

→ Employee Facilities

→ Surfaces

→ Light Fixtures

→ Aisles and Stairways

→ Spill Control

→ Maintenance

→ Waste Disposal

→ Storage

It is not uncommon for a worker to trip on a piece of equipment or tool that they themselves forgot to put away.

Why bother with Housekeeping?

Poor housekeeping can be a cause of accidents, such as:

→ Tripping over loose objects on floors, stairs and platforms

→ Being hit by falling objects

→ Slipping on greasy, wet or dirty surfaces

→ Striking against projecting, poorly stacked items or misplaced material

→ Cutting, puncturing or tearing the skin of hands or other parts of the body on projecting nails, wire or sharp protruding items.

In order to avoid these hazards, a workplace must maintain good housekeeping standards throughout the working day. Although this effort requires a great deal of management and planning, the benefits more than justify the effort.

Slippery Surfaces

One of the major causes of slips is a slippery surface. A common cause of a slippery floor is from spillages of liquids. Dusty floors resulting from work processes and from poor cleaning practices may provide another source of slippery floors. However, cleaning operations of their nature may result in the work surfaces becoming wet and slippery.

Outdoor surfaces may become slippery due to rain, sleet, snow and ice. A change from a wet to dry surface may result in slipping due to footwear losing contact with the dry surface due to a thin layer of water on the sole of the footwear.

65

Control measures that can be implemented indoors to prevent, or minimize as much as possible, injuries caused by wet outdoor surfaces include the following.

→ Anti-skid adhesive tape is an excellent and economically feasible fix to combat slips or trips.

→ During inclement weather conditions, moisture-absorbent mats should be placed in entrance areas. Caution: Improper mats can become tripping hazards themselves.

Floor mats should have bevelled edges, lie flat on the floor, and be made out of material or contain a backing that will not slide on the floor.

Have readily available and display wet floor signs.

Have a policy or procedure implemented that articulates the appropriate action to be taken when someone causes or comes across a food or liquid spill.

Where wet processes are used, maintain adequate drainage, mats, and false floors wherever possible.

Panel 6.3

Benefits of Effective Housekeeping Practices

→ Reduced handling to ease the flow of materials

→ Fewer tripping and slipping accidents in clutter-free and spill-free work areas

→ Decreased fire hazards

→ Lower worker exposures to hazardous substances

→ Better control of tools and materials

→ More efficient equipment cleanup and maintenance

→ Better hygienic conditions leading to improved health

→ More effective use of space

→ Reduced property damage by improving preventive maintenance

→ Improved morale

Unsuitable Footwear

Walking is such a common activity that little attention is paid to its potential hazards. The shoes worn can play a big part in preventing falls. The slickness of the soles and the type of heels worn need to be evaluated to avoid slips, trips and falls. Employers are required to assess the risks in the workplace and provide the correct footwear to prevent accidents and injuries.

Changes in Level

A sharp, unmarked change in level may cause a person to trip or fall. Changes in the floor level often found in workplaces include:

→ Stairs

→ Ramps

→ Steps

→ Ledges

Obstacles/Protrusions on Route ways

Injuries can also result from trips caused by reasons other than slippery surfaces, namely inadvertent contact with obstacles or other types of material (waste) and/or equipment. For example, obstacles could include obstructions across hallways, material stacked or dumped in passageways, clutter, and the

Panel 6.4

Most Common Workplace Obstructions and Intrusions:

→ Trailing cables or conduit from electrical equipment

→ Pipes

→ Hoses

→ Miscellaneous rubbish

→ Obsolete equipment

→ Door stops

→ Electrical or telephone sockets

→ Pallets

→ Storage materials

list can go on. Of course proper housekeeping in work and walking areas is still the most effective control measure in avoiding these types of hazards. Keep aisles and corridors clean, clear, and in good repair to the maximum extent possible. This is especially true in office environments where there is a common tendency to store or stack material, especially boxes, in hallways and corridors. Not only is

67

this an unsafe practice conducive to a tripping hazard but also a source of fuel in the event of a fire.

Poor Visibility

One cause of poor visibility is inadequate lighting or dirty light fittings that could prevent people seeing a slip or trip hazard such as a slope or stairwell. In addition, poor visibility may mean that people do not see warning signs. Visibility can also be affected by smoke and fumes from processes next to the walkway or by shadows caused by stacked goods obstructing lights.

Falls from a Height

Many work activities involve working at height. Working from ladders, scaffolds and platforms are obvious examples, but there are many more activities where people are required to work at height. Examples include roof work and working over tanks, pits and structures.

Falls from height are responsible for many serious and fatal injuries every year. If employees fall from a height they may sustain a serious injury. Many workers in maintenance and construction and other people in a variety of jobs, could be at risk of falling from height at work. Examples include: painters, decorators and window cleaners and those who undertake one-off

jobs without proper training, planning or equipment.

The main hazards associated with working at height are people falling, and objects falling onto people. These may occur as a result of inadequate edge protection, or poor securing of people or objects in storage.

Whilst falls are commonly associated with work in the construction industry, many occur in less risky circumstances

Whilst falls are commonly associated with work in the construction industry, many occur in less risky circumstances (e.g. Electricians fall from ladders, teachers fall from chairs and shop assistants fall when trying to get boxes down from high shelving and storage racks).

In the vast majority of cases these accidents are attributable to poor management control and not equipment failure. Commonly employers have failed to recognise a problem and have not introduced an appropriate safe system for working at height. Where there is a procedure often no checks are made to ensure that it is followed and steps are not taken to ensure that staff are provided with sufficient training and instruction.

Working at height is not restricted to those working on a roof or from a scaffold. Equally we will need to consider activities such as the use of ladders to access high shelving or carrying out window cleaning, or the storage and retrieval of items in loft areas, from flat roofs or mezzanines. Often injuries can result from use of areas, which are not structurally sound, such as fragile roofs.

All employers are required to ensure that work at height is identified and appropriately controlled, this may include removing the need to work at height altogether or providing appropriate equipment to allow work to be carried out safely. If you choose to employ contractors

Panel 6.5

Injuries can result from:

→ Any elevated work (for example, maintenance, window cleaning, installing television aerials, placing insulation in roofs, or demolition work)

→ Work near unprotected open edges of floors or roofs

→ Work near unprotected penetrations or openings in roofs, floors or walls

→ Work near unguarded shafts or excavations

→ Work associated with large vessels, such as chemical storage tanks

→ Work near or from unstable structures (temporary or permanent)

→ Work on, or near, fragile or brittle surfaces (for example, cement sheeting roofs, fiberglass sheeting roofs and skylights)

→ Work where someone could fall into water, acid or poisonous solutions

→ Work where someone could fall onto sharp or projecting objects such as exposed reinforcing steel, a picket fence, broken glass

→ Work where tools, equipment or material could be dropped onto someone below

then you also have a duty to consider the health and safety aspects of the work they carry out.

A fall from a height is most often worse than falls from ground level. Falls from height can result from a slip, trip or fall whilst working on high work platforms, mobile platforms or on roofs and ladders. Falls from a height may be caused by walking on fragile roofing that gives way or by slipping on items or ice which has accumulated on the surface of a roof.

Falls from ladders are common and can be of result of a defective rung, slipping from rungs or the ladder not been fixed securely at the ground or at the top; oftentimes scaffold ladders leave staff particularly vulnerable.

Everyone at a worksite can be at risk, whether they be a worker, a visitor to the site, a manager/ team leader, an architect or other service provider.

The behaviour of employees can also increase the risk of slipping and tripping such as:

→ Running

→ Being distracted

→ Not clearing up spills

→ General horseplay

→ Misuse of equipment

Slips, trips and falls — Risk Assessment

For slip, trip and fall risks to be adequately controlled a risk assessment should be undertaken.

All employers have to assess the risks to employees and others who may be affected by their work, e.g. visitors and members of the public. This helps to find out what needs to be done to control the risk. It is also needed to satisfy the regulatory requirements.

Controls for Slips, Trips and Falls

How can slips, trips, and falls be prevented?

Slips, trips, and falls in the workplace can be prevented using a systematic and comprehensive approach.

Managers/Team Leaders/ Employees must:

→ Be aware of slip, trip and fall hazards

→ Report any hazardous areas or conditions

→ Conduct detailed inspections of the work area on a regular basis

→ Investigate all slip, trip and fall hazard reports

→ Investigate all incident reports involving falls

→ Initiate control measures

→ Provide training

Housekeeping Inspections

An inspection of the workplace for slip, trips and falls is a common tool used to identify, monitor and control potential hazards.

Panel 6.6

Risk assessment process for slips and trips:

❶ Step 1

→ Look for slip and trip hazards around the workplace, such as uneven floors, trailing cables, areas that are sometimes slippery due to spillages. Include outdoor areas.

❷ Step 2

→ Decide who might be harmed and how. What particular employees are exposed? Who comes into the workplace? Are they at risk? Do you have any control over them? Remember that older people and people with disabilities may be at particular risk.

❸ Step 3

→ Consider the risks. How serious are the risks? Are the precautions already taken adequate to deal with the risks?

❹ Step 4

→ Record your findings – Accurately record any findings, so these items can be addressed and control measures considered.

❺ Step 5

→ Regular review of the assessment. If any significant changes take place, make sure existing precautions and management arrangements are still adequate to deal with the risks.

Panel 6.6

Housekeeping Inspections Should Cover

→ Spillages of Wet and Dry Substances

→ Floor coverings

→ Cleaning of the floor

→ Types of footwear worn

→ Wet/dirty footwear entering the building.

→ Poor Lighting

→ Unkept/Untidy Areas

→ Stairwells

→ Ramps

→ Changes in surface levels

→ Ramps

→ Storage of rubbish

→ Surface of outdoor areas

→ Ladders and other items used by people when working at a height

→ Individual/Group workload – excessive rushing/running

→ Manual Handling of loads

Management can contribute to the prevention of slip/trips by concentrating on the following areas:

➲ Areas of Access/Egress and Routeways throughout the Organisation:

→ A question should arise as to whether or not these areas are suitable for the tasks that are being carried out. Regular inspections of these areas should occur. Obvious hazards need to identified and control measured implemented.

➲ Housekeeping within the Organisation

→ A safety conscious attitude by all staff including management and employees will go a long way in removing the sources of slips, trips and falls. Where an individual notices a potentially hazardous situation, they should take the steps to correct it. An effective programme of cleaning and the provision of an adequate number of rubbish bins is also required. Suitable and adequate areas must be provided for safe storage.

➲ Building Design and General Maintenance

→ The entire building and its structure should not add to the risk of slips, trips and falls occurring. The size and design of the routeways, exits, entrance points and stairwells etc should be adequate for the tasks and people using them. Where an issue has been brought to light, the repair/ maintenance should be swift to prevent possible incidents. The use of preventative maintenance programme is commonly used to prevent possible accidents occurring, for example — changing light bulbs in walkways so as to ensure that adequate lighting will be provided for those using the walk way, thereby visibility in this area will be adequate.

Summary of Chapter 6

→ Slip, Trips and Falls are often one of the biggest hazards found in organisations. The movement of people, goods and equipment can contribute to accidents

→ A number of local factors can contribute to accidents occurring — Poor Housekeeping, Wet/Slippery Floor, Poor Visibility or Wearing the wrong footwear can contribute to accidents

→ Protrusions where people walk are a major source of trip hazards — trailing cables, pipes, rubbish, bags, door stops and floor sockets are examples found in many organisations

→ Many serious accidents involve falls from a height. This can range from a great height (scaffold), to someone falling a short distance (step up ladder). Both are serious hazards that can result in serious life threatening injuries

→ Behaviours such as running, horseplay or misuse of equipment can increase the risk of Slip, Trip and Fall accidents

→ Controlling Slip, Trip and Fall Hazards includes Risk Assessments and Inspections

→ Improvements in areas such as Housekeeping/Maintenance, Access/Egress and Building Design will aid in preventing accidents from slip, trip and fall hazards

Fire Safety
Management

7

Chapter outline
Fire Safety Management

→ Introduction
→ The Fire Triangle
→ Fire Prevention
→ Fire Fighting Activities
→ Fire Hazard Identification
→ Assessing and Reducing the Risk of Fire
→ Summary

Introduction

Definition of Fire

Fire can be defined as the resulting heat and light energy released during a chemical (combustion) reaction. Depending on the substances alight and any impurities within; the colour and intensity of the flame may vary.

Fire Triangle

Fire is a chemical reaction. It involves 3 essential ingredients shown in the fire triangle below:

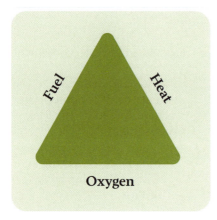

Fire Prevention

Fire prevention is based on preventing the three elements of the fire triangle coming together thereby preventing the occurrence of Fire.

It is important for the manager to identify all sources in each of the categories of the fire triangle.

Fuel sources will include all and everything in your business that can burn, not just fuel bought with that intention.

→ Furniture and fittings

→ Paper, cardboard and packaging

→ Flammable materials/ chemicals/gases

→ Wiring

→ Structural materials

→ Clothing

→ Food items

→ Waste

List all potential sources of **heat**:

→ Ignition sources - mobile phones, sparking tools, friction

→ Open flames - hot work, furnaces, bunsens, welding, cutting

→ Grills, hot plates, heaters, radiators, pipe work, boilers

→ Mirrors/glass

List all potential sources of **oxygen**:

→ Ambient air

→ Oxidising materials which can release oxygen

→ Air conditioning systems

Once the above have been identified within the three elements organisations must:

→ Try to eliminate as many as possible from your operation

→ Replace with safer substitutes, for example fire retardant non-flammable materials

Fire Fighting Activities

Reducing the risk of fire

Once managers have identified the risks it is necessary to put in place some or all of the methods of reducing risks that are listed below:

→ Compartmentalise, through utilising:

  − Fire doors, fire breaks, fire corridors, fire curtains

→ Fire suppression systems, such as:

  − Sprinkler systems

  − Automatic suppression systems;

→ Risers ...wet/dry

→ Water reservoir/tanks

→ Fire fighting equipment and trained users

→ Emergency plans

  − Escape routes

  − Fire Alarms

  − Emergency lighting

  − Evacuation procedures

  − Fire Drills

Fire Arrangements

For effective management of fire hazards, the employer or occupier of an organisation's building should comply with the following requirements:

→ Carry out a Fire Risk Assessment

  → Provide and maintain, to the extent that it is appropriate as determined by the Risk Assessment:

    − Means for Detecting and Giving Warning in Case of Fire

    − Means of Escape and Emergency Lighting

    − Fire Safety Signs

    − Firefighting Equipment

→ Monitor and review the Risk Assessment and revise as appropriate

→ Inform staff and their representatives of the risk

→ Plan for an emergency

→ Provide staff information and training

→ Nominate persons to lead and assist

For a fire to occur it needs sources of heat and fuel. If these hazards can be kept apart, removed or reduced, then the risks to people and your premises is minimised. In order to do this you must first identify fire hazards in your workplace.

Fire Hazard Identification

◉ **Identify Any Combustibles -** These can be divided into two main groups, combustible fuels such as paper, wood, cardboard, and highly combustible fuels such as Thinners, Solvents and Polyurethane Foam, among other items.

◉ **Identify Any Sources of Heat** - All workplaces will contain heat/ignition sources. Some will be obvious such as cooking equipment or open flames (heating or process); others may be less obvious such as heat from chemical processes or electrical equipment.

◉ **Identify Any Unsafe Acts -** Persons undertaking unsafe acts such as smoking next to combustible materials even when some are located outside the premises.

◉ **Identify Any Unsafe Conditions -** These are hazards the may assist a fire to spread in your workplace, in situations, for example where there are large areas

of hardboard or polystyrene tiles among other materials. Open stairs that can cause a fire to spread quickly, trapping people and involving the whole building or sections of same.

Assessing and Reducing the Risk of Fire

The manager/team leader must consider the risk to any people who may be present, employees and visitors. There will, however, be some occasions when certain people may be especially at risk from the fire, because of their specific role, disability, sleeping, location or the workplace activity. You need to consider matters carefully if:

→ Sleeping accommodation is provided

→ Persons are challenged, for example physically, visually, mentally

→ People are unable to react quickly

→ Persons are isolated

Attempt to classify each area as 'high', 'normal', or 'low risk'.

Low Risk – Areas where there is minimal risk to people's lives, where the risk of fire occurring is low, or the potential for fire, heat and smoke spreading is negligible and people would have plenty of time to react to an alert of fire. **Normal Risk** – Such areas will account for nearly all parts of most workplaces. These are areas where an outbreak of fire is likely to remain confined or spread slowly, with an effective fire warning allowing persons to escape to a place of safety.

Having identified the hazards you need to reduce the chance of a fire occurring and spreading

High Risk – Areas where the available time needed to evacuate the area is reduced by the speed of development of a fire, through highly flammable or explosive materials being stored or used (other than small quantities under controlled conditions). Also where the reaction time to the fire alarm is slower because of the type of person present or the activity in the workplace, such as the infirm, elderly or persons sleeping on the premises.

If the building has been built and maintained in accordance with Building Regulations and is being put to its designed use, it is likely that the means of escape provisions will either be adequate, or you will be able to decide easily what is required in relation to the

risk. Having identified the hazards you need to reduce the chance of a fire occurring and spreading, thereby minimising or removing the possibility of harm to persons in the workplace by:

→ **Removing** the hazard altogether

→ **Reducing** the hazard to the point where there is little or no risk

→ **Replacing** the existing hazard with a safer alternative

→ **Segregating** the hazard from the workplace

→ **Developing a Prevention Policy and Culture** to ensure hazards do not occur in the workplace. This should be a dynamic assessment, involving pre-planning if introducing new processes or working practices and appropriate control measures being put in place.

Matters you will also have to consider are:

→ **Means for Detecting and Giving Warning in Case of Fire** - Can it be heard by all occupants; does it need to be automatic in operation?

→ **Means of Escape** - Are they adequate in size, number, location, well lit, unobstructed, safe to use

→ **Signs** - for exits, fire routines, equipment

→ **Firefighting Equipment -** Wall mounted by exits, suitable types for hazards that are present and sufficient in number?

Arrangements for warning all occupants in the event of a fire

A fire starting in any location should not be allowed to go undetected and reach a size that could cause persons to become trapped.

must be adequate and failsafe. Fire alarm systems, smoke detectors and alarms, hand bells or a single shout may be suitable depending on the size and complexity of the workplace. Arrangements should be made to ensure a telephone is available in a place of safety in order to call the Fire Service in the event of fire.

Escape, predominantly without the use of a key, should be possible from all parts of a workplace to a place of safety in fresh air normally within two-and-a-half minutes, if the premises are considered 'high risk' this should be undertaken in much less time.

A fire starting in any location should not be allowed to go undetected and reach a size that could cause persons to become trapped. This is more likely to happen where there is only one way out of an area. Ideally, persons should be able to turn their back on a fire and walk in the opposite direction towards the fire exit(s), although the lay-out of some premises may not allow this. If your workplace is small and the fire risk has been assessed as normal or low then there may be no need to have alternative ways out but where your escape is in one direction only, the dead end areas should be kept as short, as few, and as low risk as possible.

Recording Fire Assessment Details

When carrying out a fire assessment the findings and the required actions (including maintenance) should be recorded; you must retain a record which may be in writing, or by electronic or other means. It should indicate:

→ The date the assessment was made

→ The hazards identified

→ Any staff and other people especially at risk

→ What action needs to be taken, by whom and by when (Action Plan)

→ The conclusions arising

Prepare the Emergency Plan - The aim of the plan is to ensure that in the event of fire everyone, including contractors and casual employees are sufficiently familiar with the action they should take; also and that the workplace can be safely evacuated to a location where persons will not be in danger. The employer is responsible for preparing the plan, and in most small workplaces this should not be difficult, and it may simply take the form of a Fire Action Notice.

Training - All staff should receive induction and regular training relating to the action(s) to be taken in case of fire in particular evacuation procedures, fire extinguisher training, where appropriate; this induction should also take account of any specialist duties assigned such as calling the Emergency Services or assisting disabled persons to safety. Escape routes should be walked regularly and an evacuation drill practised at least annually. Visitors and contractors should also be informed of relevant procedures, in particular evacuation and other matters such as permits to work. Some employees may be selected as Fire Wardens and specialist training should be sought for these employees to fulfill their duties correctly.

Monitor and Review on a Regular Basis

The fire risk assessment is not a once-off procedure. It should be continually monitored to ensure that the existing fire safety arrangements and risk assessment remains realistic.

The assessment should be reviewed if there is a significant change:

→ In the occupancy

→ Work activity

→ The materials used or stored when building works are proposed

→ Young persons are employed

→ When it is no longer thought to be valid

→ An annual review should take place, irrespective of whether or not there are changes.

Summary of Chapter 7

→ An outbreak of fire within a building can have catastrophic consequences for life and the company's business

→ It is essential that Managers play their part in Fire Prevention

→ Fire involves 3 ingredients – Fuel, Heat and Oxygen. In order to prevent fire, one of the 3 ingredients must be removed

→ Management must assess their workplace and identify potential fire hazards

→ Try to eliminate the sources or replace with less dangerous – non-flammable or fire retardant

→ Management need to also take account of other factors in the risk assessment – if people sleep in the building, people who may be visually, mentally or physically challenged, people with poor reactions or isolated persons

→ Managers or Occupiers of buildings must install fire fighting equipment and organise fire fighting measures

→ Management must also monitor and review the procedures in place on a regular basis to ensure that the fire safety arrangements operate successfully

Manual Handling in the Workplace

Chapter outline
Manual Handling in the Workplace

→ Introduction
→ Definition of Manual Handling in the Workplace
→ Risk Factors
→ Manual Handling Risk Assessment
→ Controlling Manual Handling Risks
→ Summary

Introduction

It is estimated that over a third of all reported occupational accidents are as a result of manual handling activities. The risk from manual handling injuries is present in most occupational settings and wherever people work across all organisations and sectors.

An employer must consider the risks from manual handling to the health and safety of his/her employees. If risks are present in your workplace, then there are usually national regulations that also apply to the control of risk from manual handling in the workplace, with which you will need to comply.

Only a very small number of manual handling injuries are caused by lifting heavy weights.

Remember at all stages it is important to consult with your employees and their representatives as they know their jobs best and therefore will know the risks best. They may also be able to define the best solutions to controlling the risks.

In general employers are required to:

- ➔ **Avoid** – the need for hazardous manual handling (so far as is reasonably practicable)

- ➔ **Assess** – the risk of injury from manual handling that cannot be avoided

- ➔ **Reduce** – the risk of injury from manual handling (so far as is reasonably practicable)

Definition of Manual Handling in the Workplace

Manual Handling involves more than just the lifting and/or carrying of heavy weights. It can include any activity requiring the use of force exerted by a person to lift, push, pull, carry or otherwise move or restrain any moving or stationary object.

The load may be either inanimate for example a box or a trolley; alternatively that to be moved may be a person or animal.

Only a very small number of manual handling injuries are caused by lifting heavy weights. Often, seemingly simple activities such as repetitive reaching, twisting and bending, as well as poor sitting, standing and typing postures can contribute to an injury occurrence.

Risk Factors

Extensive research has been undertaken to identify workplace risk factors much of which has focussed on the development of back injury, which is the most frequent injury arising from manual handling. Legislation will require the employer to take into account any risk factors stipulated, when carrying out risk assessments on manual handling activities. The aim is that the employer will be able to identify the risk factors present in the activity being assessed.

The most common risk factors which must be taken into account by managers are:

→ The Characteristics of the Load

→ Physical Effort Required

→ Characteristics of the Working Environment

→ Requirements of the Activity

→ Individual Risk Factors

It is important to remember that a combination of risk factors can be identified in any one activity.

The Characteristics of the Load

There are no specific requirements such as weight limits that an individual can lift or move. However, there are some numerical guidelines available which take into account weight, repetition and location of lift as means of identifying tasks that involve risk.

The person carrying out the risk assessment must take into account the nature of the work and have an appreciation of what reasonably practicable improvements can be introduced to avoid or reduce the risk e.g. the introduction of mechanical aids, which may not always be possible.

Weight is not the only factor that needs to be considered. Other factors such as repetition, individual capacity, working posture and work environment should also be considered. Examples include:

→ The load is too large to see over

→ The load is unwieldy or difficult to grasp

→ The load is unstable or has contents likely to shift

→ The load has to be held at a distance from one's body trunk

→ The load itself is harmful, for example hot or sharp

→ The load is awkwardly stacked

As previously mentioned, numerical guidelines for weights can be used to determine if a load is too heavy. Working outside of these guidelines is likely to increase the risk of injury. Work, from a weight lifting view point, should be made less demanding if it is reasonably practicable to do so.

Physical Effort Required

A physical effort may present a risk if for example the physical effort is:

→ Too strenuous

→ Involves twisting movements (especially of the trunk of the body)

→ Likely to result in sudden movement

→ May be made with one's body in an unstable posture

Managers should ensure that they regularly assess the risks associated with physical effort.

Characteristics of the Working Environment

Certain characteristics of the working environment may increase risk if, for example:

→ Insufficient room (confined space) to safely move in (vertically and horizontally)

→ Constraints on posture

→ Bumpy, obstructed or slippery floors

→ Variation on levels of the floor or the working surface requiring the load to be manipulated at different levels

→ Unsuitable temperature, humidity or ventilation

→ Poor lighting conditions

→ Clothes or personal protective equipment which restrict movement.

It is important for managers and team leaders to regularly review the working environment on issues such as the above.

Requirements of the Activity

The activity may present a risk if it involves one or more of the following:

→ Overly frequent or over prolonged physical effort involving the spine

→ Insufficient bodily rest or recovery period

→ Excessive lifting, lowering or carrying distances

→ A rate of work imposed by a process which cannot be altered by the employee

→ Large vertical movements

→ Holding loads away from the body

Employees should play their part in bringing to the attention of managers/team leaders specific requirements of the activities associated with their work.

Individual Risk Factors

The employee may be at risk if he or she:

→ Is physically unsuited to carry out the task in question

→ Is wearing unsuitable clothing, footwear or other personal effects

→ Does not have adequate or appropriate knowledge or training.

→ Is in a job that requires unusual capability e.g. above average strength or agility

→ Has an existing health problem or is challenged physically or mentally

→ Is pregnant

All these risk factors need attention from managers and team leaders; the rewards of such attention will be less accidents and injuries.

Manual Handling Risk Assessment

Manual Handling Risk assessment can be described as a system which involves:

→ Gaining a detailed understanding of a task

→ Collecting all relevant technical data of the task

→ Identifying if there are risk factors present

→ Determining what solutions are available to reduce or eliminate the risk factors

→ Implementing a plan to introduce the control measures.

Ideally risk assessments should be completed as part of the design of a process so that measures can be taken to reduce or eliminate the risk factors at that design stage.

Most assessments will be able to be completed in-house. Remember that you and your employees know the business better than anyone else. Advice and guidance from external agencies/experts may be helpful in unusual or difficult issues.

The risk assessment should take into account the following factors:

→ Actions and movements

→ Workplace and workstation layout

→ Working posture and position

→ Duration and frequency of manual handling

→ Location of loads and distances moved

→ Weights and forces

→ Characteristics of loads and equipment

→ Work organisation

→ Work environment

→ Skills and experience

→ Age

→ Clothing

→ Special requirements

→ Any other factors considered relevant by the employer, the employees or their representatives on health and safety issues

→ The Risk Factors earlier identified

Risk must be reduced to the lowest level that is reasonably practicable, which means, reducing the risk until the cost of any further precautions — time, effort or money — would be far too great in proportion to the benefits.

Effectiveness is the degree to which the control measures have avoided or reduced the risk of injury.

All risk assessments should be formally recorded. The purpose of the assessment is to outline the areas that require attention. They will also allow you to prioritise, with higher risk activities taking initial priority. It is also important to remember to update the assessments when significant changes have been made to the workplace in order to reduce or eliminate the risks. Employees should be made aware of the risk assessments that apply to them.

Care should be taken to ensure that further risks to health and safety are not created by the application of control methods aimed at the reduction of manual handling risks.

For each issue identified in the risk assessments it is necessary to evaluate the controls that are feasible. The rationale for agreeing on each control measure must be documented thus outlining why other control measures were not possible and how the agreed control measure will avoid or reduce the risk of injury to employees.

It is advised that a plan of action be implemented to identify what changes are planned to allow staff time to adjust to the changes and to communicate all of the changes to the relevant personnel.

Consultation is very important at this stage, ensuring that all interested parties are working as a team to decide if the recommended controls are practical; also to gain feedback on other possible controls and to ensure the full implementation of the plan of action.

It is also very important to review the effectiveness of the implemented control measures. Effectiveness is the degree to which the control measures have avoided or reduced the risk of injury. This will depend on how timely the changes were implemented and the level of worker acceptance.

A critical period is the time before the risk factor is reduced or eliminated. This includes the time required for the control measure to effectively work where, for example, a change in work methods or procedures is involved. Whether or not workers accept and use the proposed solution is a key measure of the effectiveness of a control measure.

Controlling Manual Handling Risks

As an employer you must ensure so far as is reasonably practicable that the risks associated with manual handling are controlled. Remember that risk control must be done in consultation with employees and their representatives.

Risk control is the process of eliminating or reducing identified and assessed risk factors and can be best accomplished through a combination of:

→ Job re-design

→ Mechanical handling equipment

→ Provision of training

→ Administrative/managerial controls

Job Re-design

The key to job re-design is eliminating or reducing three risk factors — force, repetition and body posture. There usually are a number of variables for which there will be no quick and easy solutions.

Risk control is the process of eliminating or reducing identified and assessed risk factors

There a number of ways to achieve job re-design, as shown below:

Where manual handling has been identified as a risk the employer should:

→ Re-design the manual task to eliminate or control the risk factors, and

→ Ensure that employees involved in manual handling receive appropriate training, including training in safe manual handling techniques

Where re-design is not practicable, the employer should ensure that the following are put in place:

→ Adequate training in methods of manual handling appropriate for that manual handling task and training in the correct use of the mechanical aids.

→ Personal protection equipment.

→ Team lifting procedures.

→ Re-design workplace and workstation layout through installing an adjustable platform to reduce bending and reaching.

→ Modify how objects are moved/handled through storing heavier objects at waist level which will make them easier to move.

→ Change the object to be lifted/handled by changing the shape of bulky objects or using smaller cartons.

→ Reduce forces required by reducing body movements such as lifting, twisting, reaching, holding or bending.

Mechanical handling equipment

There is a wide range of mechanical handling equipment and aids available to reduce or eliminate the risk from manual handling activities. Some examples include:

→ Belt conveyors

→ Cranes

→ Hoists

→ Trolleys

→ Pallet Trucks

→ Fork lift trucks

→ Barrel Lifters

Managers should ensure that if mechanical handling equipment is introduced that it is risk assessed to ensure that it will not introduce further risk.

Provision of Training

Wherever a risk from manual handling exists for employees, the organisation must provide adequate training in safe manual handling techniques to the exposed employees, regardless of their position in the organisation.

Ideally the training should promote an understanding of methods to avoid risk in manual handling. As earlier mentioned, training should also be provided in the use of mechanical aids, team lifting and personal protective equipment as required.

Administrative/Management Controls

Administrative/Management controls do not control the source of the risk from manual handling. They usually change personnel arrangements and will only reduce a person's exposure. Common examples include:

→ Manual Handling Policy

→ Signs

→ Posters

→ Job Rotation

→ Preventative Maintenance on mechanical equipment used

Administrative/Management controls are often used as short term measures while planning and budgeting for more expensive design controls is undertaken.

Summary of Chapter 8

→ People are inclined to think that Manual Handling involves only lifting or carrying weights, but it also includes activities such as pushing and pulling.

→ Risks of a manual handling injury are found in most workplaces and can occur from a range of activities.

→ Employers have a legal duty to assess the manual handling risks to which employees are exposed

→ The risk assessment should cover all the risk factors.

→ Workplaces may have the following risk factors that may contribute to manual handling injuries – Characteristics of the Load, Physical Effort Required, Characteristics of the Working Environment, Requirements of the Activity and the individual themselves.

→ After risk factors have been identified – management must consider what can be done to eliminate or reduce the risks as far as is reasonably practicable.

→ Controlling the risks can be achieved with a combination of Job Re-design, Introducing Mechanical Equipment to aid lifting, pushing and pulling and the provision of manual handling training.

9 Display Screen Equipment

Chapter outline
Display Screen Equipment (DSE)

→ Introduction
→ Display Screen Equipment (DSE)
→ DSE Hazards and Injuries
→ DSE Assessment
→ Benefits of DSE Assessment
→ Training of Assessors and Users
→ Summary

Introduction

Display Screen Equipment (DSE) is any work equipment having a screen that displays information. Typical examples are computer screens often called monitors or VDUs (visual display units).

The term for DSE generally excludes:

→ Drivers' cabs or control cabs for vehicles or machinery

→ Computer systems on board a means of transport

→ Computer systems mainly intended for public use

→ Portable display screen equipment not in prolonged use at a workstation

→ Calculators, cash registers and any equipment having a small data or measurement display required for direct use of the equipment

DSE Hazards and Injuries

Hazards of DSE work include:

→ Work related upper limb disorders (WRULDs)

→ Temporary eye strain and headaches

→ And fatigue/stress

Work Related Upper Limb Disorders (WRULDs)

WRULDs covers a wide range of injuries resulting from:

→ Highly repetitive movements

→ Movements requiring excessive force

→ Movements at the extremes of reach

→ Rigid and awkward postures

Sometimes, just one of these factors may cause the injury. More frequently, it's a combination. These are also referred to as Repetitive Strain Injuries (RSI).

These range from temporary fatigue or soreness in the limbs, to cramp, to on-going pain in the muscles or nerves. Holding a part of the body rigid for a long time such as the back, neck and head may cause discomfort in the muscles, bones and tendons. Awkward positioning of the hands and wrist relative to the work being carried out is another likely factor.

These effects can be avoided by using proper equipment, suitable furniture, training and changing the way in which the work is carried out.

99

Panel 9.1

Stages of WRULDs conditions

➔ **Mild:** Pain, aching and tiredness of the wrists, arms, shoulders or neck during work, which improves overnight. This stage may last weeks or months, but is reversible.

➔ **Moderate:** Recurring pain, aching and tiredness occurring earlier in the working day, persisting at night, and perhaps disturbing sleep. Physical signs may be visible, such as swelling of tendon areas. This stage may last several months and may only be reversed with difficulty.

➔ **Severe:** Pain, aching, weakness and fatigue are experienced even when resting completely. Sleep is often disturbed and the sufferer may be unable to carry out even light tasks at home or work. This stage may last for months or years. Sometimes it is irreversible and full use of the affected part may never be regained.

Effects on the Eyes

Some employees may experience temporary eye fatigue, with such symptoms as failure to see clearly, red or sore eyes and headaches. Eye fatigue may also lead to employees adopting awkward postures which may cause discomfort of the limbs. Medical evidence shows that using VDUs does not cause damage to eyes or eyesight, nor does it make existing defects worse.

Panel 9.2

Eye fatigue may be caused by:

→ Staying in the same position and concentrating for a long time

→ Poor positioning of the VDU

→ Poor legibility of the screen or source documents

→ Poor lighting, including glare and reflections

→ A drifting, flickering or jittering image on the screen

While using a VDU does not cause eye damage, it may make employees with pre-existing vision defects, which have not been corrected, more aware of them. Such uncorrected defects may make working with a VDU more tiring or stressful than would otherwise be the case. Employees using a VDU as a habitual part of their work, should be afforded the opportunity of an eye examination for VDU usage.

Fatigue and Stress

The volume of VDU work to be carried out by employees can vary widely between different employments and activities. The work may range from air traffic control to accounting, stock recording and control, or documentation creation and revision. Some tasks may require a very high degree of concentration and vigilance. More routine tasks can even give rise to boredom. Some tasks can result in stress or fatigue.

People who use a VDU sometimes complain of stress/fatigue, but this usually arises from increased pace of their work or pressure to meet deadlines, not the VDU itself. Some VDU workers find stress reduced because the VDU makes their job easier or more interesting, but for others stress becomes worse. This can happen when a system does not work well or when the user does not feel in control or competent to operate it.

DSE Assessment

DSE Assessments should be carried out by all organisations for users of VDUs. Controlling DSE risks in the workplace involves assessing workstation ergonomics, environmental conditions and the duration and intensity of the tasks. All these factors should be taken into account so that the risks can be reduced to the lowest level reasonably practicable. Training and information about the risks of working with DSE should be provided to each individual by the assessor.

The principle of workstation ergonomics is to ensure that the task is adapted to the worker, not the worker to the task. The assessment will adjust the workstation to ensure the employee is sitting with the correct posture and in a safe comfortable position. From this it is felt that the employee will not only be in a safe seating position but this will also aid productivity.

An assessment will examine the following:

→ Chair

→ Display screen

→ Keyboard

→ Work desk

→ Desk (reaching,etc.)

→ Screen (glare)

→ Lighting

→ Noise

→ Heat, humidity and radiation

Panel 9.3

Benefits of DSE Assessment

→ Allow the employer to meet legal requirements

→ Provides management with an understanding of design problems or underlying engineering/ventilation problems of the individual(s) workstations or office

→ Reduces the risk of RSI or Work Related Upper Limb Disorders (WRULDs) injuries and eyesight problems

→ Provides staff with a safer and more beneficial working environment

→ Reduces stress and fatigue factors related to the work environment

→ Allows the employer to identify and put in place any extra training and information that may be required for employees

Training of Assessors and Users

DSE assessors are required throughout your organisation to perform a more detailed risk assessment if such a need is identified following self-assessment by the user. A sufficient number of suitably qualified persons need to be appointed and trained, specifying for which work area/location and workstations they are responsible.

DSE assessors should be competent in the following:

→ Understanding the national legislation appropriate to walking with DSEs/VDUs

→ Understanding the principles of office safety and recognising unsafe work layouts, environments and practices

→ Ensuring that the job/task being assessed is designed to enhance the employee's efficiency

→ Assessing the layout and design of the workstation equipment and installation so that they can be operated safely and effectively

→ Ensuring that work conditions and work equipment are organised to promote correct body posture

→ Ensuring that work systems permit adequate rest periods and facilities for changing posture, to fulfil a person's basic need for movement

→ Drawing conclusions as to the risk of injury and identifying where, and what type of corrective action is required

→ Deciding when more information and help is needed and knowing who to contact

→ Communicating the findings of the assessment to appropriate personnel

DSE Users

Operators and users must be adequately trained and informed on all aspects of health and safety relating to their workstations.

Panel 9.4

Training should cover the following:

→ The use of adjustment mechanisms on equipment, particularly items of furniture so that stress and fatigue can be minimised

→ The use and arrangement of the individual parts of the workstation to enable good posture, prevent over-reaching and to avoid glare and reflections on the screen

→ The need for regular cleaning or inspection of screens and other equipment for maintenance

→ The need to take advantage of breaks and changes of activity

→ The use of software

Summary of Chapter 9

→ Display Screen Equipment (DSE) is found in every organisation. It is essentially work equipment that has a screen that displays information, often called Visual Display Units (VDUs) or monitors

→ Hazards from working DSEs include - Work Related Upper Limb Disorders (WRULDs), Temporary eye strain and headaches, fatigue and stress

→ WRULDs are commonly called Repetitive Strain Injuries which result from highly repetitive movements, awkward postures, using excessive force or movements involving excessive reach

→ Common WRULD Injuries include – Tendonitis, Carpal Tunnel Syndrome or Burstitus. WRULD symptoms build up over a period of time and can be mild to severe

→ Eye fatigue can result in failure to focus, sore red eyes or headaches. Prolonged use, poor posture, equipment in poor condition and bad environmental conditions can contribute

→ Stress and Fatigue can be related to a number of factors at work....also to non-work related situations

→ Employers should acquire the services of a qualified DSE Risk Assessor to identify hazards, assess the risks and introduce control measures

→ The assessment will cover the workstation ergonomics, environmental conditions, duration and intensity of the tasks

→ The results of the assessments should lead to more comfortable, productive and safe DSE use

Managing
Work-related Stress

10

Chapter outline
Managing Work-related Stress

→ Introduction
→ Definition of Stress and Work Related Stress
→ Sources of stress
→ Effects of stress
→ Prevention of Workplace Stress
→ Management of Stress at Work
→ New Approaches to Stress Management
→ Summary

Introduction

Definition of stress and work related stress

Stress is a state, which is accompanied by physical, psychological or social complaints or dysfunctions and which results from individuals feeling unable to fulfil the requirements or expectations placed on them.

Generally people are able to cope with short-term exposure to pressure, which can be considered as positive, but have greater difficulty in coping with prolonged exposure to intensive pressure. Moreover, different individuals can react differently to similar situations and the same individual can react differently to similar situations at different times of his/her life. Stress is not a disease but prolonged exposure to it may reduce effectiveness at work and may cause ill health.

Often there is no single cause of work-related stress. Although it can be triggered by sudden, unexpected pressures, it's often the result of a combination of stressful factors that build up over time.

Stress originating outside the working environment can lead to changes in behaviour and reduced effectiveness at work. All manifestations of stress at work cannot be considered as work-related stress. Work-related stress can be caused by different factors such as work content, work organisation, work environment, poor communication and organisation climate among other things.

Sources of Stress

Given the complexity of the stress phenomenon, it is difficult to provide an exhaustive list of potential stress indicators. However, high absenteeism or staff turnover, frequent interpersonal conflicts or complaints by workers are some of the signs that may indicate a problem of work-related stress.

Identifying whether there is a problem of work-related stress can involve an analysis of the workplace. There are a number of factors that can make employees feel stressed at work, including:

→ Training and career development. A failure to provide employees with opportunities for career development, and adequate training for their job or career may promote stress.

→ Failure to provide workers with significant autonomy and control over their day-to-day work tasks can promote stress. Trusting workers and 'empowering' them to make decisions is more likely to promote a positive response than if management attempts to control everything.

→ Work intensification, long hours, and tight deadlines. Workers may become stressed when they feel they have no control over work pace, they work excessive hours, or they are under significant pressure to meet deadlines.

→ Poorly defined and designed work roles and tasks may cause stress. Clearly defined work roles, and variation in work tasks within work roles, are likely to alleviate stress.

→ Irregular work schedules. Unpredictable work schedules, particularly frequent changes in shiftworking, may cause stress.

→ Workers in insecure, casual forms of employment are more likely to suffer stress

→ Poor interpersonal relationships with individuals in management or with colleagues

→ Poor work environment. Physical features of the work environment, such as poorly designed workspace and poor ventilation, may promote stress.

→ An inadequate work-life balance. The failure to accommodate employee's interests and responsibilities outside the workplace is a significant cause of stress

→ Insufficient staffing levels

→ Exposure to workplace restructuring and rationalisation

→ Employees who are bullied, harassed or isolated, and who do not feel supported by managers or colleagues, may experience stress.

However, often there is no single cause of work-related stress. Although it can be triggered by sudden, unexpected pressures, it's often the result of a combination of stressful factors that build up over time. If a problem of work-related stress is identified, action must be taken to prevent, eliminate or reduce it. The responsibility for determining the appropriate measures rests with the employer.

Effects of Stress

The effects of stress on workers can take many forms and may depend on a number of different reasons. The main effects of somebody experiencing some form of stress are:

➔ Physical

→ Sleep disturbances

→ Headaches

→ Gastrointestinal upset

→ Raised blood pressure/ cardiovascular disease

⊜ Emotional

→ Anxiety and irritability

→ Depression

→ Instability

⊜ Intellectual

→ Loss of concentration

→ Lack of motivation

→ Difficulty with thought process

→ Loss of memory

→ Poor decision-making

⊜ Behavioural

→ Substance (including alcohol) misuse

→ Decreased libido

→ Inappropriate display of behaviour

→ Isolation

→ Poor Time Keeping

⊜ Effects on the organisation may include:

→ High absenteeism

→ High labour turnover

→ Poor time keeping

Panel 10.1

Prevention of Work Related Stress

There is a moral requirement for employers (and in many countries a legal requirement) to assess the working environment for systems and practices which lead to stress and to put in place preventative measures.

Policies which benefit employee health can improve productivity. Low levels of perceived stress are associated with low staff turnover, low levels of absenteeism and low rates of injury. Organisations that are perceived as healthy tend to have clear policies and active methods of dealing with people which encourage:

→ Respect for the dignity of each employee

→ Regular feedback and recognition of performance

→ Clear goals for employees in line with organisational goals

→ Employee input into decision- making and career progression

→ Consistent and fair management actions

→ Poor performance and productivity

→ Low morale

→ Poor motivation

→ Increased employee complaints

→ Increased ill-health, accidents and incidents reports

Management of Stress at Work

There are three main types of stress management interventions used in organisations – Primary, Secondary and Tertiary.

⊖ **Primary Interventions** (Prevention) This approach looks at the issue of stress 'at source', in order to prevent it occurring. It usually involves some form of organisation-wide change in the system of work, be it the design of how things are done, what is done and/or who does what.

⊖ **Secondary Interventions** (Management) This approach focuses on the employee throughout his or her period with the organisation. It includes aspects of work such as training for the job and training in aspects of health and safety; it is also important to provide support in terms of providing adequate management of the social and technical aspects of an employee's working life. This good management practice has a role both in preventing stress and helping stressed employees to recover.

⊖ **Tertiary Interventions** (Minimisation) This focuses on the provision of counselling and employee assistance programmes or outsourced support services in order to assist employees who feel a need for extra support, other than that contained in the Human Resource function.

A combination of all these interventions is generally advisable, rather than focusing solely on any one to the exclusion of all others.

Management of Stress (Risk Assessment)

⊖ **Identify** the hazards (causes of stress) – what are the aspects of your organisation that have the potential to cause stress?

⊖ **Assess the risks** – prioritise them according to severity and likelihood of negative outcome

⊖ **Eliminate the risks** – change the system so that the stressful aspect of work is eliminated

⊖ **Contain the risks** – limit the impact of and/or reduce the number of causes of stress

⊖ **Protect from the risks** – reduce the degree of exposure to the factors that cause it

➜ **Monitor the risks** – on-going review of levels of stress in your organisation

Management Impact

More importantly, as a manager you have a huge impact on the work-related stress of your employees. For instance:

Managers must take account of the stress-related issues that we have raised with the objective of providing a working environment that will be as stress free as possible.

→ You can prevent (or conversely cause) stress by the way that you behave towards your employees

→ Your influence may mean employees can be protected from, or exposed to, stressful working conditions, for instance negotiating an extension to a deadline in a team that is already working to full capacity

→ Working closely with your team, you are well positioned to identify stress in others at an early stage

→ If one of your employees suffers from stress, you, as their manager, are likely to be involved in the solution

→ As a manager, your position is paramount to the success of work development or change initiatives

→ Finally, increasingly managers are responsible for the uptake and roll-out of risk assessments for work stress within their team or department.

New Approaches to Stress Management

Recent studies and reports have concluded that new approaches to the organisation and management of work would appear to be required, in order to prevent and eliminate stress. These include:

→ Designing stimulating jobs that provide workers with variety and allow them to use their creativity and skill; this may incorporate various forms of job rotation and job enrichment

→ Reducing close management control and providing workers with greater autonomy over their own work, and involving them in decisions that affect their jobs

→ Consulting and communicating openly with workers at different levels on a regular basis

→ Making sure that workers have some prospect of career development and providing them with adequate training

→ Making sure that workers have an adequate balance between their work responsibilities and their interests and responsibilities outside work. Employee-friendly flexible forms of working are likely to be important here, as are childcare provisions

→ Managing and organising work in a coherent and competent manner, so that workers have clear roles and know what is expected of them

→ Organising work to allow employees to interact with their peers

→ Making sure that work pressure is not too intense, allowing workers to control the pace at which they work, and avoiding setting unrealistic deadlines and targets.

Managers must take account of the stress-related issues that we have raised with the objective of providing a working environment that will be as stress free as possible.

Summary of Chapter 10

→ Like any other hazard, stress requires intervention from management to identify sources, assess these risks and place control measures to eliminate or reduce risk to a level that is as low as is possible

→ High absenteeism, staff turnover, regular conflict or complaints at work are indicators of a possible problem of Work Related Stress

→ Common sources of stress for employees include: Career Development, lack of autonomy, intensive work — deadlines, long hours, badly organised work, and irregular work patterns — shift work

→ Stress can affect individuals in different ways, typically symptoms are displayed as Physical, Emotional, Intellectual, Behavioural

→ Stress can also have detrimental effects on the company which can manifest itself in: increased absenteeism, poor performance or attention, low morale and poor motivation, to mention just a few

→ Management have moral duty to address all stress related issues in the workplace

→ Organisations should develop a clear policy on stress management

→ The intervention of management in preventing workplace stress is essential, as it is usually management that can address the sources of stress and make the appropriate decisions to eliminate or reduce it

Preventing
Bullying at Work

11

Chapter outline
Preventing Bullying at Work

→ Introduction
→ Definition of Bullying
→ Bullying prevention policy
→ Communication of the Policy
→ Training and Supervision
→ Bullying prevention measures
→ Resolving bullying at work
→ Summary

Introduction

As we have seen throughout this book, management have the responsibility of providing a safe and healthy environment at work. This responsibility extends to ensuring that the environment is free from bullying and/or harassment.

Bullying at work can be a significant cost for both employers and employees, in both financial and human terms. If bullying is not dealt with and resolved internally, it can lead to employers being brought before outside agencies or the courts. If bullying behaviour is tolerated within an organisation it affects the performance and general health and well being of individuals and/or the workforce. The effects of bullying can linger for a considerable length of time both for individuals and the organisation.

Stress, ill health, loss of confidence and self-esteem and career difficulties can result for the victim(s). For the employer, a dysfunctional workplace, reduced productivity, poor morale, lost time, industrial relations problems and the threat of litigation can follow.

Bullying at work can involve staff in many different work situations and at all levels:

→ Manager/Team Leader to employee

→ Employee to Team Leader/ Manager

→ One employee to another (or group to group)

→ Customer or business contact to employee

→ Employee/Team Leader/ Manager to customer/business contact.

Panel 11.1

Definition of Bullying

There have been many debates as to what workplace bullying actually is. It has been defined as 'repeated inappropriate behaviour, direct or indirect, whether verbal, physical or otherwise, conducted by one or more persons against another or others, at the place of work and/or in the course of employment, which could reasonably be regarded as undermining the individuals right to dignity at work'.

What Bullying is Not!

Employers have a right to direct and control how work is done and managers have a responsibility to assess workflow and provide feedback on performance. If a worker has performance problems, these should be identified and dealt with it in a professional manner that does not involve personal insults or derogatory remarks. The following are some examples of work situations that do not constitute workplace bullying:

Panel 11.2

Sample Behaviours and patterns of workplace bullying

→ Exclusion with negative consequences

→ Verbal abuse/insults

→ Physical abuse

→ Being treated less favourably than colleagues

→ Intrusion — pestering, spying or stalking

→ Menacing behaviour

→ Intimidation

→ Aggression

→ Undermining behaviour

→ Excessive monitoring of work

→ Humiliation

→ Withholding work-related information

→ Repeatedly manipulating a persons job content and targets

→ Blame for things beyond the persons control

→ Mobbing

→ Harassment

(This is not an exhaustive listing)

→ An isolated incident of inappropriate behaviour e.g. a conflict of views

→ Fair and constructive criticism of an employee's performance, conduct or attendance during the course of performance reviews or at other times

→ Legitimate management responses to crisis situations

→ Complaints which should be dealt with under the normal grievance procedure

Bullying Prevention Policy

Prevention is the best method of avoiding the risk of bullying in the workplace. An effective clear policy and a commitment to implementing it are essential. The aim of the policy should not only be to prevent improper conduct and behaviour but also to promote best practice and a safe healthy workplace where such behaviour is less likely to occur.

The commitment must come from the top and be seen to be so.

Preparing a Bullying Prevention Policy

The policy must apply to everyone, from the most senior person in the organisation to temporary employees. It must state clearly that bullying is a disciplinary offence which is linked to existing disciplinary procedures.

It is important that the policy is formulated, signed and dated by a person in a senior managerial role in the organisation.

Prior consultation should take place with all interested parties (e.g. directors, managers, staff, safety representatives, union representatives) and agreement should be sought regarding the formulation and implementation of the policy. This will be the first step in creating an anti-bullying culture. It is advisable that formal records be maintained of this consultative process.

It is important that the policy is formulated, signed and dated by a person in a senior managerial role in the organisation. The policy should be regularly reviewed and updated when appropriate.

Simple direct language should be used in the policy. It is important that the information given is in a form, manner, and language that is reasonably likely to be understood by all employees.

It is important to remember to write the policy in accordance with local legislative requirements or codes of practice that may apply.

Panel 11.3

Communication of the Policy

It is vital that the existence of the policy is made known to everyone in the workplace. This can be achieved by:

→ Giving each employee a copy

→ Including the policy in staff bulletins, newsletters, leaflets, websites, emails, staff handbooks and notice boards.

→ Explaining it in training courses and training manuals

→ Including it in the recruitment and induction process

Failure to do most of the above leaves organisations open to the claim that employees were not aware of the policy.

Training and Supervision

All employees must be provided with information, training and supervision to ensure the prevention of bullying in the workplace. This should include:

→ Making every employee aware of the existence and content of the Bullying Prevention Policy

→ Managing/Team Leading one's work area to ensure a climate free from bullying

→ Information of the appropriate behaviour in compliance with the terms and conditions of the policy

→ Training if required on compliance with the policy

→ Assistance if necessary to overcome a bullying incident

A well-run training course should identify the factors which contribute to a bullying free working environment and will remind trainees of their responsibilities outlined in the policy. Training is crucial for supervisory staff, for staff responsible for implementing the policy and for those involved in responding to complaints. It is necessary to ensure that all training is documented.

Bullying Prevention Measures

Role Clarity

Employers must define each employee's role and accountability as clearly as possible. This may include a written description of main duties and responsibilities and a clear line of supervision for each employee. This should be reviewed on an on-going basis and any changes in job content should be communicated clearly to the individual and those working alongside him/her.

Defining Responsibility

Managers and Team Leaders have a responsibility to manage in such a way as to protect the safety, health and welfare of employees. This includes the responsibility for preventing bullying at work and for the resolution of alleged cases of bullying at work.

Also, every employee is responsible for their own safety, and that of their colleagues who may be affected by his/her actions, while at work. Therefore, every employee has a duty not to place the safety and well being of colleagues at risk by engaging in bullying.

Access to Advisory Services/ Contact Person

A 'contact person' should be named in the Bullying Prevention Policy. This person can listen and advise about complaints of bullying at work and give an explanation of the procedures in place to resolve them. This 'contact person' must receive appropriate training.

Situations may arise as regards workplace bullying where an organisation may benefit from expert assistance.

The contact person is appointed to this role, oftentimes following staff consultation. Their role is a voluntary role to act as the first point of contact for someone who believes that he or she is being treated in a manner that could amount to bullying. The contact person is not an advocate for either party, and provides a listening brief and reference point for the complainant.

Situations may arise as regards workplace bullying where an organisation may benefit from expert assistance. This can be sourced externally through employer representative bodies, trade unions or from relevant

Panel 11.4

Informal Responses to a complaint that alleges bullying

→ An employee who believes they are bullied should, if possible, advise the perpetrator that their behaviour is unacceptable. Where this is not possible the complainant should seek advice from the contact person nominated in the Bullying Prevention Policy. The contact person will act as the initial facilitator for the complainant

→ Initial complaints maybe verbal or written. If it is communicated verbally it is recommended that very little if anything is put into writing, as the issues get harder to solve once put in writing. An internal mediated approach may be the best alternative at this stage

→ It is then important to determine a course for resolution so that both parties can return to a professional working environment free from bullying. This is best done initially through mediation

public bodies. It may also involve the services of persons particularly qualified in mediation or counselling or training in this area.

Resolving Bullying at Work

The majority of policy recommendations suggest a two-tier approach to resolving bullying complaints – an informal stage and then, if the informal stage is not sufficient or the alleged offence is of a serious nature, a formal stage. Both stages should be outlined in the Bullying Prevention Policy and must be followed and implemented if and when a complaint is made.

Informal Stage

On receipt of a complaint, the employer should first strive to have the issue resolved informally with the consent of the parties involved.

Intervention

The first step is to gather all the facts of the complaint, the specific issues complained of, when they occurred and to make a decision whether or not they fall within the definition of bullying (as per the Bullying Prevention Policy).

Where it has been identified, steps to halt the bullying behaviour, should be agreed with both parties, along specified lines.

A programme may be introduced to change behaviour or it may involve mediation by an agreed mediator who is experienced with dealing with bullying in the workplace. If such mediation appears to resolve the issues then the parties should sign up to the new values and behaviours that are agreed and a review mechanism that facilitates the review of on-going relationships.

The designated person should keep records of all stages. The purpose of keeping these records, is proof of evidence of the complaint having been met with an organisational response and attempt at resolution. All records should be filed, stored and managed as per local Data Protection laws.

Closure

It is important to obtain closure after a resolution is achieved through informal procedures. Each party should be provided with support and reviews, which if necessary could include counselling or other appropriate interventions and/or support services.

Where a complaint has been assessed as without reasonable or probable cause or excuse and thus vexatious, the matter may proceed through disciplinary procedures.

In the majority of situations, with the co-operation of all parties involved, the matter can rest here.

Panel 11.5

Natural justice for Respondents is generally considered to include the right to

→ Be fully informed of the complaint against the person accused, including being told the name of the person making the complaint and receiving any relevant documentation

→ Respond in full to the complaint

→ Be considered innocent until the due process is concluded

→ Representation by a person of his or her choice

→ Have information about the complaint restricted to those who are directly involved

→ Be given the benefit of any reasonably doubt

→ Have all mention of the matter removed from his or her personal records if the case against him or her is not proven

Formal Stage

A formal process should also be in place and described in the Bullying Prevention Policy, including its aim and objectives along with the procedures and time frames involved. This should also be accompanied by a statement of support to those involved in the process (complainant and the respondent).

The formal process should be used if a complaint cannot be resolved through the earlier described informal process. The formal process will include a formal complaint process and a formal investigation process.

Formal Investigation

The terms of reference outlined in the Bullying Prevention Policy should be followed when carrying out the investigation including the time scale for completion and the scope of the investigation.

Statements must be recorded from all parties in writing. Copies of all statements made should be agreed and provided to the person making the statement by the investigator.

The person conducting the investigation of the complaint should be:

→ A designated member of management

→ An external third party if deemed appropriate

The Investigator should also be familiar with the Bullying Prevention Policy, and investigate the complaint thoroughly, objectively and with sensitivity, maintaining the confidentiality and respect for the rights of all parties involved. Each person involved, when they have been interviewed by the Investigator, must be given the right to be represented by a union representative or a colleague.

When the investigation is completed the Investigator should submit a report that should include his/her conclusions and Determination. Each party involved should be given a copy of the report, and given time to submit comment, before the employer decides on actions to take, if any.

If any actions are to be taken by the employer, he/she must inform the parties involved of these actions.

Natural Justice

Natural justice must be observed in all dealings with those accused of workplace bullying. It is crucial that people be protected against false and malicious accusations. Persons may be falsely accused of workplace bullying because of

→ Attempts to resolve earlier performance issues

→ An overreaction to some trivial incident

→ A desire to harm the accused person

Furthermore, false accusations can be part of the bullying process in itself and people could be accused of bullying as a means of covering up bullying by someone else.

Also, it is important to afford these rights of natural justice as, if same are denied, then any action taken against him or her may be overturned should he/she appeal against it. Therefore he/she escapes punishment even if the original accusation was correct.

Summary of Chapter 11

→ The management of health and safety is the Employer's responsibility. This responsibility also extends to preventing and resolving bullying at work

→ Bullying in the work place can take many forms – repeated inappropriate behaviour, direct or indirect verbal, physical or other behaviour which may undermine an individual's right to dignity at work

→ To prevent B&H occurrences a definitive B&H prevention policy showing management's commitment to same should be developed

→ The policy must apply to everybody and during its development consultation between all parties should take place

→ The policy will set out how the organisation will deal with any allegations or accusations of B&H. Everyone in the organisation shall receive a copy

→ A two tier approach to resolving cases of bullying is encouraged. This approach involves firstly going through the Informal Stage and, if this does not work, the Formal Stage can then be utilised

→ Organisations should make every effort to resolve B&H issues at the informal stage

→ The Rights of Natural Justice should be afforded in **full** to both parties

A more in-depth treatment of Bullying and Harassment can be seen within another book in this series

Bullying & Harassment – *Values and Best Practice Responses*
By Frank Scott-Lennon & Margaret Considine